A Practical Guide to Property
For Under 40s

A Practical Guide to Property for Under 40s

Copyright © Paul Argus, 2018

Paperback ISBN: 978-0-6480769-7-1

First published 2018

Photographs sourced with permission from www.istockphoto.com

Published with the assistance of loveofbooks.com.au

Disclaimer

**Let's get the legal stuff
out of the way up front.**

The author does not make any representation or warranty about the accuracy, reliability, currency or completeness of any material contain herein.

This guide is based on the author's personal experiences and opinion, you should exercise your own independent skill and judgement before relying on it. This guide is not a substitute for independent professional advice and readers should obtain appropriate professional advice relevant to their particular circumstances.

The material in this guide may incorporate or summarise views, statistical data or recommendations of third parties or comprise material authored by third parties ('third party information'). The author makes no representation or warranty about the accuracy, reliability, currency or completeness of any third party information.

The author does not take responsibility for any loss resulting from any action taken or reliance made by you on any information or material including, third party information herein contained. All CoreLogic data is used with permission of the owner and is bound by their standard copyright and disclaimers. The views and opinions expressed in this book are those of the author and do not necessarily reflect the views, policies or position of any companies associated with the author.

Reproduction of the contents of this book is expressly prohibited. You may not make or distribute unauthorised copies of the book, or use, copy, modify, or transfer the book, in whole or in part, unless you receive the Author's express permission.

In loving memory
of Fran Pope

1936 - 2017

About the Author

At the age of 26 Paul purchased his first property in South Auckland, New Zealand, pooling his money together with his brothers and stepfather. A second in West Auckland followed a year later. Paul and his wife have subsequently added four more properties to their portfolio across Auckland and Sydney, making their first sale in 2016 to help fund their dream home.

His professional career in marketing and as a strategist has encompassed both banking (ANZ and Commonwealth) and property sectors (CoreLogic and Key Exchange). He managed ANZ Bank's home buyer segment in New Zealand before making the move to Sydney in 2008 to run mortgage marketing for Commonwealth Bank, co-leading the creation of the Property Guide iPhone application, a collaboration of CBA and CoreLogic which is still used by over half a million Australians. During this period Paul's work was recognised across the globe on 48 occasions including the Cannes International Festival of Creativity, Caples Awards, the Global Festival of Media and the Effies. His work has also been referenced by the likes of Forrester, Deloitte, the World Advertising Research Centre and JWT Top 100.

CoreLogic (formerly known as RP Data) are the largest property data company in the world. They support many of the decisions real estate agents, banks and brokers make when valuing a home or approving a mortgage. Paul has been working with them via his company Paul & Co, since 2011. He lead the creation of CoreLogic's Property Value, offering a combination of free and subscription-based information and tools for home buyers and property investors.

Paul currently resides in the Northern Beaches of Sydney, Australia with his wife Brady and three children Emily, Finn and Piper.

Contents

CHAPTER ONE
Intro

1 Why I wrote this guide
2 Capital growth, bubbles and affordability

CHAPTER TWO
Buying

17 That pesky deposit
20 Everything is compromise
24 Property stats
30 Buying
32 Thinking one step ahead

CHAPTER THREE
Selling

36 Selecting an agent
37 Price and commissions
40 Selling methods
43 Preparing your home for sale
45 Offers and settlement

CHAPTER FOUR
Renovating

48 Renovating appropriately

CHAPTER FIVE
Finance

58 Mortgage interest rates
64 Compounding interest
68 Loan to value ratios
70 Brokers
73 Refinancing

CHAPTER SIX
Equity

79 Equity
80 Property investing

CHAPTER SEVEN
Advice

92 Paying for invaluable advice

CHAPTER EIGHT
Conclusion

99 Is property for everyone?

CHAPTER NINE

102 Glossary

CHAPTER ONE
INTRO

Why I wrote this guide

The idea to create this book actually came from my wife. She had noticed a number of friends asking for my thoughts on which property to buy or how much to pay, as well as wanting advice on their mortgage. I guess it's no different to asking your stockbroker friend for market tips, or your tradie mate to help you build a deck, but at the time I didn't really think of it that way. I do however remember being surprised by how many of our well-educated friends weren't aware of what people in the industry see as 'the basics'.

As I've written this guide, housing affordability in Australia and New Zealand has continued to slide – where many people under 40 have almost given up on the idea of owning a home. Conversely, there are a large number of people convinced these markets are 'bubbles' about to burst, ready to swoop in and capitalise on the carnage that will follow and pick up property at 50% of its current value.

The truth is, while there are tools to help you make better decisions, no one really knows how the market will perform or what interest rates will do. However, while government is able to influence via changing policies, there are financial and market fundamentals that never change and people will continue to buy and sell property in up and down times. I also believe there is hope for the current generation of 'under 40s'. So whether you're looking to invest, buy your first or next home, or simply repay your mortgage faster, there are always options to increase your ability to achieve your property goals.

This guide takes a high level view of a wide range of topics relating to property. I hope it gives you at least one practical learning you can apply to your personal situation, and then pass this and your own experiences on to your children.

Cheers

Paul

Capital growth, bubbles and affordability

What you need to know.

It's true that for most of us our property goal is simply having something to call our own regardless of how much its value changes. However, I've started with capital growth because it's one of the most important aspects of buying and owning property and a key factor in affordability.

Capital growth relates to the increase in value of a property over time. The current value of a property is compared to the amount originally paid for it - presented as a percentage.

For example:

2012: Property purchased for $500,000
2016: Property valued at $600,000
Capital growth: ($600,000 - $500,000)/$500,000 = 20%

Positive capital growth is great for owners as it represents a gain in their net wealth because the property value has increased. It's also important for potential buyers providing a reference point for what they might expect to pay to live in a particular area. When growth is high it affects affordability, restricting the number of people who can enter the market.

But it can be negative too. You've probably heard about 'property bubbles' in Australia and New Zealand. This relates to capital growth being faster than what is sustainable and property becoming 'overvalued'.

This puts the growth bubble at risk of 'bursting' with property values going backwards quickly. This has happened before in countries including America and Ireland.

Despite many predictions, as at August 2017 Australia and New Zealand are yet to experience this 'market correction' despite the widening gap between household income and property values.

Bubbles (or at least rapidly increasing property prices) have a larger impact on those who buy close to the peak (before it pops) as they are at risk of their property becoming worth less than they paid for it. In some cases their mortgage can be higher than the value of their property. If they need to sell for any reason that loss is realised in their pocket rather than 'on paper'.

So how can you tell if a property market is 'overheated' or 'experiencing bubble-like growth'? One of the best measures is to work out how 'affordable' it is to own a property in the city and surrounding suburbs you work in. Affordability is calculated by comparing property values to household income – presented as a ratio.

For example if the median price is $800,000 and the median household income is $80,000 then the ratio is 10:1.

Demographia creates an annual International Housing Affordability Report looking at housing (not unit) affordability across a number of countries. They consider a ratio of 5:1 or more to be 'severely unaffordable' and a ratio of 3:1 or below 'affordable'. So they're saying, for example, if your household income is $120,000 you really shouldn't pay much more than $360,000. I personally think the definitions are on the conservative side and if you really want a property you probably need to stretch yourself and go without some things, but the report provides a great guide.

Ratio = Median[1] price / Median Income	

Affordable	3.0 and under
Unaffordable	3.1 to 4.0
Seriously Unaffordable	4.1 to 5.0
Severely Unaffordable	5.1 and over

Source: Demographia International
1: The median is similar to the average, but simply orders all of the numbers from highest to lowest and takes the middle number

The first chart from the 2017 Demographia report given below shows each of the listed markets which have ratios above three, meaning they are 'unaffordable' (using their definition). Hong Kong aside, New Zealand stands out given its unaffordability is not limited to one or two cities.

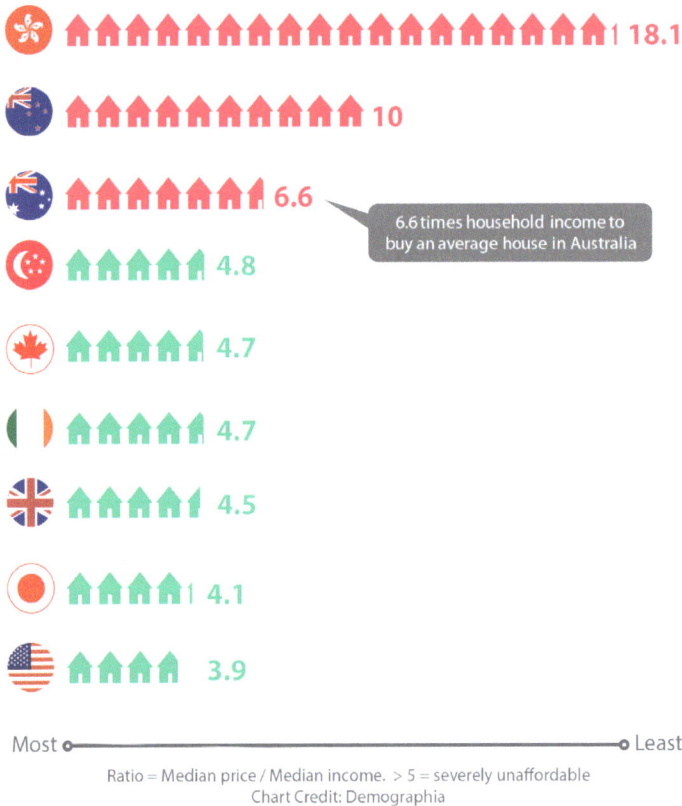

🏠🏠🏠🏠🏠🏠🏠🏠🏠🏠🏠🏠🏠🏠🏠🏠🏠🏠 18.1

🏠🏠🏠🏠🏠🏠🏠🏠🏠🏠 10

🏠🏠🏠🏠🏠🏠 6.6

6.6 times household income to buy an average house in Australia

🏠🏠🏠🏠🏠 4.8

🏠🏠🏠🏠🏠 4.7

🏠🏠🏠🏠🏠 4.7

🏠🏠🏠🏠🏠 4.5

🏠🏠🏠🏠 4.1

🏠🏠🏠🏠 3.9

Most ●━━━━━━━━━━━━━━━━━━━━━━━━━● Least

Ratio = Median price / Median income. > 5 = severely unaffordable
Chart Credit: Demographia

The picture is worse when looking at the least affordable cities, all of which are major centres. Sydney, Auckland and Melbourne are all classified as 'severely unaffordable', well above a ratio of 5.1.

Least Affordable Cities

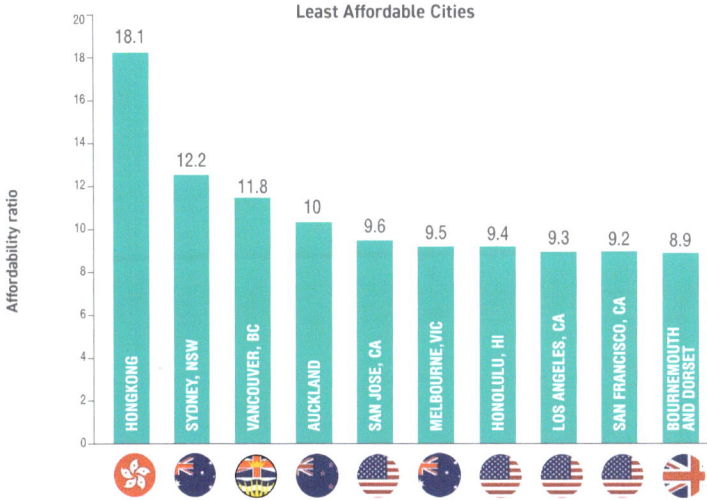

City	Affordability ratio
HONGKONG	18.1
SYDNEY, NSW	12.2
VANCOUVER, BC	11.8
AUCKLAND	10
SAN JOSE, CA	9.6
MELBOURNE, VIC	9.5
HONOLULU, HI	9.4
LOS ANGELES, CA	9.3
SAN FRANCISCO, CA	9.2
BOURNEMOUTH AND DORSET	8.9

Chart Credit: Demographia

It's still possible to find major housing markets (populations of 1 million or more) with a ratio of three or less, but in United States markets which are generally characterized by more liberal land use regulation.

Most Affordable Cities

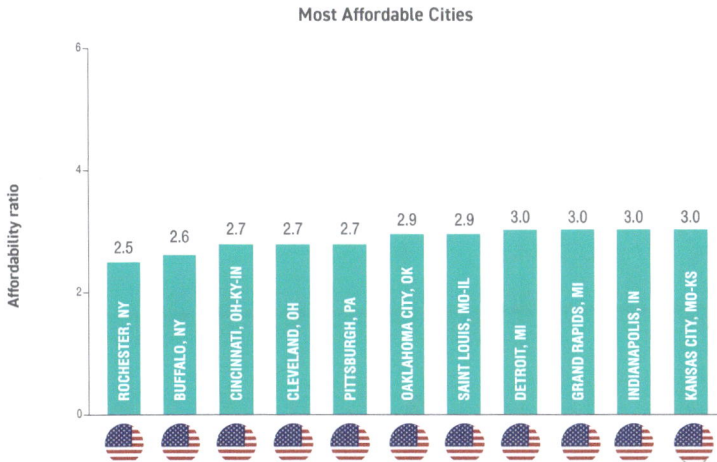

City	Affordability ratio
ROCHESTER, NY	2.5
BUFFALO, NY	2.6
CINCINNATI, OH-KY-IN	2.7
CLEVELAND, OH	2.7
PITTSBURGH, PA	2.7
OAKLAHOMA CITY, OK	2.9
SAINT LOUIS, MO-IL	2.9
DETROIT, MI	3.0
GRAND RAPIDS, MI	3.0
INDIANAPOLIS, IN	3.0
KANSAS CITY, MO-KS	3.0

Chart Credit: Demographia

Some cities may be alot more affordable, but you also need to consider the economy and employment prospects

What makes places like Buffalo and Cincinnati different to Sydney and Auckland? Buffalo has been experiencing a population decline for the better part of 50 years and the economy and job outlook has only recently improved[2]. Cincinnati has experienced similar population declines.

Compare this to Auckland (population 1.4 million) which increased by 20,000 people a year without anywhere near that much housing being added. Australian markets are also forecast to continue their healthy population growth post 2017.

Having said that, there is more to Australia and New Zealand than just Sydney, Melbourne and Auckland. Many other cities and major centres offer different lifestyle benefits at greater affordability (albeit still at ratios considered 'severely unaffordable'). The chart below summarises some of these.

Affordability - AU and NZ Cities

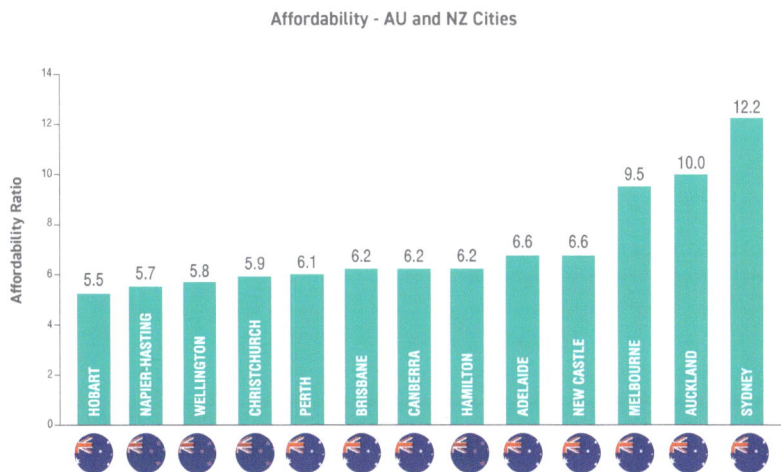

City	Affordability Ratio
HOBART	5.5
NAPIER-HASTING	5.7
WELLINGTON	5.8
CHRISTCHURCH	5.9
PERTH	6.1
BRISBANE	6.2
CANBERRA	6.2
HAMILTON	6.2
ADELAIDE	6.6
NEW CASTLE	6.6
MELBOURNE	9.5
AUCKLAND	10.0
SYDNEY	12.2

Chart Credit: Demographia

2: https://en.wikipedia.org/wiki/Buffalo,_New_York

The objective is to get on the property ladder (most likely near the bottom)

Moving to the United States not an option?

If you're reading this guide, you're probably living in Australia or New Zealand and have no intention of moving to Buffalo. But I believe there is hope for first home buyers:

1 As you learned earlier, the 'median' is the middle and a first home buyer shouldn't expect to buy a property in the middle of the pack. The objective is to get on to the property ladder (most likely near the bottom) which will involve compromise. You'll learn more about compromise in the context of property in the next chapter.

2 It's important to note that the Demographia research looks at houses, not units. While units aren't everybody's first choice, they are more affordable due to the efficient use of land and are often located in convenient locations near city centres. We will continue to see increasingly more unit and apartment living.

3 Additionally, while ratios of ten or more are clearly unaffordable I do believe that buying a property requires you to financially stretch a little outside of your comfort zone. It's unrealistic to buy your first home and enjoy the same lifestyle.

4 As discussed earlier, there are many major centres in Australia and New Zealand that offer good employment and lifestyle options without the price tag of the Auckland, Melbourne and Sydney. I would expect to see more people moving to these areas and balancing commuting with flexible work hours.

Will affordability improve in these locations?

We know why these cities are expensive, but will they ever become affordable again? Well, the one thing most experts agree on is that rapid capital growth is not sustainable. Some of the reasons it happens are (relatively) strong economies, historically low interest rates, increased immigration and not enough new housing. A lower interest rate really helps increase the amount you can borrow. Add in working mums and it's a perfect cocktail for the banks who have generally been happy to lend the money (although this changed significantly around 2016 as the Australian and New Zealand Governments attempted to slow things down).

The population growth for the most popular locations in Australia and New Zealand is forecast to continue, albeit at slower rates placing continued pressure on housing stock and greater demand for employment.

	GROWTH[1]	2014 POP (,000)	RANK	2034[2] POP (,000)	RANK	2054[2] POP (,000)	RANK
SYD	1.50%	4,840.6	1	6,432.6	1	7,966.4	2
MEL	1.95%	4,440.3	2	6,238.1	2	7,982.4	1
BNE	1.92%	2,274.6	3	3,340.6	4	4,406.6	4
ADL	1.06%	1,304.6	5	1,604.7	5	1,843.7	5
PER	3.05%	2,021.2	4	3,451.8	3	4,923.0	3
HBA	0.67%	219.2	7	250.4	7	266.6	7
DRW	2.30%	140.4	8	175.5	8	212.6	8
CBR	1.70%	386.0	6	N/A	6	N/A	6

[1] - Annual population growth rate between 2009 and 2014.
[2] - Estimated based on medium levels of fertility, overseas migration, life expectancy and interstate migration flows.

Chart Credit: McCrindle.com.au

A lot of large companies are trimming their workforce to reduce costs. If you lose your job and can't find another quickly, the first thing you do is sell, right? That's fine in a buoyant market, but if everyone is selling at the same time supply goes up and suddenly buyers have the power. This reduces sale prices and leads to (in some cases) negative capital growth (a reduction in property values) and improved affordability (for those who are employed).

The other factor driving property growth has been foreign investment, often from Chinese investors wanting to move their money to what they see as a 'safe haven'. While this has been proven to not be as significant as the general public might think, it has certainly had an impact. This is now showing signs of easing, further balancing the supply and demand ratio.

So will affordability improve? I believe growth in Australia and New Zealand will absolutely hit a wall - it simply has to. However, there are ways to manage this and although no one knows the future I have some confidence in government policies to allow a softer landing, balancing the needs of existing owners and those priced out of the market. Despite what the public might think there are some very clever people working at the Reserve Bank.

Heading for a soft landing?

Usually on social media someone will make a claim that the property market is going to lose 50% or more of its value overnight. This is a possibility but for me there are enough tools and general behaviour changes to manage this over a number of years, spreading the correction out and somewhat improving affordability. Why?

- Growth rates in 2017 slowed, albeit not as quickly as people would like and I see them tending to be flat to slightly negative over the next few years (flat growth is effectively backwards when you factor in inflation at 2 - 3%)

- I think we'll see a continuation of 'multi speed markets' where Sydney, Melbourne, Auckland will fare better than traditionally less popular areas which will decline first

- I think it's likely there will be a significant correction in apartment values (10% or more) in areas where there has been significant development of supply in the past few years

- Interest rates have been at historically low levels, and while I don't think they are likely to change drastically there is a strong possibility they will increase by 2% or more (for example 4% to 6%) towards 2020

- Overall I don't see median values being much different (+/- 10%) in five years time to what they are now. If we look back at historical examples of this, Sydney prices didn't move much for five years between 2004 and 2009. As wages rise with inflation affordability will improve

How will we get there and how does it help me buy a home?

Banks:

1. Australian and New Zealand banks are requesting both higher deposits and interest rates from investors, dampening speculation.

2. I think a key reason for growth was buyers stretching themselves to the limit and not factoring in higher interest rates. This allowed them to increase their budgets and pay more. The banks are now testing whether an applicant can afford to repay based on higher future interest rates than they have modelled previously.

3. Interest rates reached historical lows throughout 2016 and 2017 and they are unlikely to stay that low forever. While it seems counter intuitive for higher interest rates to help first home buyers, the impact this has on property values will mean a lower required deposit and smaller mortgage. Many people that are priced out of the market can actually afford the mortgage repayments, but don't have the required deposit to make the initial purchase.

Governments:

4. The May 2017 Federal budget in Australia imposed a number of measures, largely attempting to slow speculator and foreign investment appetite:

   - First home buyers will be allowed to salary sacrifice contributions for a home deposit (limited to $30,000 per person and $15,000 per year)

   - An annual foreign investment levy of $5,000 on all foreign investors who leave their properties vacant for at least six months per year

   - Removal of main residence capital gains tax exemption for foreign investors (meaning they will be subject to a tax bill when they sell the property at a profit)

   - Restoring requirements preventing developers from selling more than 50% of new developments to foreign investors

5. Immigration, while still net positive, is being tightened, reducing pressure on housing demand and aiming to ease unemployment.

Lifestyle:

6. Increasingly people are seeing value in regional areas and commuting. I personally know a number of people who live in the Central Coast or South Coast areas and commute into Sydney on the train, clearing their emails during the journey and/or working from home. Others in Auckland, New Zealand are commuting from an hour or more outside the CBD.

7. People in Europe often rent for their entire lifetime, due in part to laws which provide the tenant with more rights than they have in Australia and New Zealand, but also because of the freedom it offers (no mortgage!). I think the great home ownership dream will still exist, but not to the same extent, opening up increased investment in other areas such as the share market and entrepreneurship.

While it might make sense to hold off jumping into the property market for a few years, property often comes with an emotional connection. For those with young families, waiting might not be helpful. So, if you're struggling to get into the market you really have two choices:

· Place your bets on a sudden market correction (and hope it's a big one that happens soon)

· Consider the above factors, do your homework and compromise...

CHAPTER TWO
BUYING

20%

That's generally how much of the purchase price you need to save before you can get a mortgage.

That pesky deposit

The initial barrier to your first home.

Saving $50,000 can be unachievable for many people, but you need at least this (ideally double) to get a small foothold into the property market in Australia and New Zealand, especially near major cities.

While forgoing your weekly smashed avocado and annual holiday is helpful, its unlikely to get you that deposit anytime soon. Realistically you need to take a five year view and break it down into weeks, $200 at a time. If you're partnered up and both working this may be feasible but for singles and couples on lower incomes it's very difficult.

Even if you do scrape a deposit together or are lucky enough to be gifted it you still need to make the mortgage repayments so you'll probably need to get creative.

That's where pooling your funds with others should become a consideration because it shares the repayments and the initial deposit.

Property Share?

Teaming up with family or friends? Yes it's fraught with risks given you need to guarantee each other's loans, however with the right paperwork up front you can significantly cut the impact of those risks. I bought my first two properties this way by teaming up with my two brothers and stepfather giving me a 25% share. It wasn't much but then I didn't need a large deposit either, and all of the weekly costs were manageable. We still have one of the properties and a long term tenant. As rent has increased over time we don't need to put any extra money in so it just ticks along growing in value with the mortgage decreasing bit by bit.

Seven tips for sharing:

1 Give a lot of consideration to who you'll be teaming up with. Look at how much you trust them and consider their personalities (are you likely to clash when making decisions etc.).

2 Take a long term, conservative view and make sure everyone is on the same page. Aggressive, short term approaches are likely to place more pressure on the group. 2017 marks our 13th year.

3 Agree up front how much each person can afford to contribute to the deposit and work to the lowest amount. It should also be decided how much each person can afford for monthly bills and if you aren't living in it any shortfall between rent and mortgage repayments.

4 Have a legal document written up clearly stating shares and voting rights, then agree how voting will work. In our case (four people) we decided that three being in agreement was enough to make a decision.

5 Get a property manager. They are worth their weight in gold and can act as an independent view when you need it.

6 Go in with the view that you don't personally own the property. Instead think of it as a business. Where possible, share the workload of administration and maintenance.

7 Be open to letting people exit either by buying them out or selling the property. Holding someone hostage is unlikely to end well. If you've held the property long enough you will have enough equity[3] for the bank to refinance the property without others having to put further funds in.

3: Equity is the difference between the value of an asset and what you owe on it.
For example, a property worth $500,000 with a $300,000 mortgage has $200,000 equity.

Take a five year view and break it into weeks, $200 at a time

If you're not up for sharing a mortgage but can afford a 2 bedroom property you can rent a room out. We had international students stay with us for a couple of years and it helped a lot. I appreciate it's not ideal but it doesn't have to be forever. Alternatively, we have friends who permanently advertise their spare bedroom on Air BnB, in addition to the entire apartment when they go away for the weekend.

Also worth pointing out is Australia has 'stamp duty' on property purchases, increasing considerably with the purchase price. There are concessions for lower value properties and first home buyers but you'll need to factor this on top of your deposit.

Everything
is compromise

Y es it's a cliche but compromise couldn't be more relevant to property. Every decision you make will involve weighing up imperfect options.

Unit or house?
Owner occupy or rent?
Inner city capital gain or regional suburb yield?
Basic or top end renovation?

It's never been tougher for first home buyers, especially when many work in the inner city and naturally want to limit their commute time. The thing is big cities in countries like Australia and New Zealand grew so much between 1995 and 2016 that there is increased pressure on housing. The baby boomers didn't have to cope with this, but still compromised and did it paying 15% interest rates for a while.

My wife and I have managed to secure above average incomes, so I appreciate we have an advantage, especially with a double income.

We also bought our first home before values increased dramatically. However, we still compromised every time we purchased. For example, we wanted to continue living in Manly, NSW and also have a house with a big outdoor area for the kids. We simply couldn't afford it. Watching our minimum budget get blown away by baby boomer opening bids at auctions proved that quickly enough.

We'd also worked our way up to this point - my first purchase was in my home town of South Auckland which isn't exactly known for its prestigious lifestyle.

$$\triangle$$

Price

Location   Size/Quality

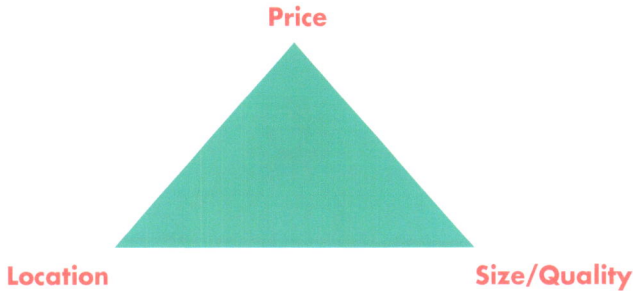

A good way to help you understand compromise is to imagine a triangle with three factors you are considering. You can have any two, but not all three. The example above has the factors a good price, great location, and a nice big house (size/quality). If price isn't a concern, you can have a large quality home in the best location.

For the other 99.99% of us we generally need to compromise on either location or size/ quality. The level of compromise is relative to income, so while higher income earners shouldn't be 'complaining', it should be acknowledged they also need to consider the triangle.

In our case, as soon as we prioritised land size over location we won the next auction we attended (in Queenscliff, NSW). This is the next suburb up from Manly so we didn't actually move that far, but the house was a

complete knock down and the size of land was moderate. If we had compromised more on location we could have purchased a nicer home on a bigger block for a similar price, but we felt the home was the right purchase for us.

The very first home we purchased together (in New Zealand) backed onto a major motorway off ramp. Of course this will impact the price we get if we ever sell but it allowed us to purchase it in the first place.

We also compromised when we purchased our unit in Manly. Having grown up living in houses in New Zealand, it took a lot to 'settle' for a unit, but at that point in our lives we prioritised the location. This meant not only did we buy a unit but it was completely 1970s original. I still remember friends seeing it for the first time and doing their best to say something nice.

```
                          Price


                          /\
                         /  \
                        /    \
                       /      \
                      /        \
                     /          \
                    /            \
                   /              \
                  /_____\
      Location                        Occupy
```

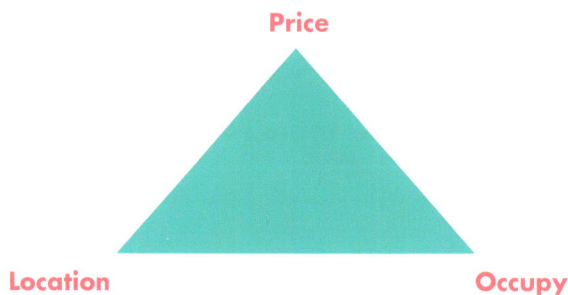

We renovated and sold it for almost twice the price five years later. This was largely due to market growth but also the renovation potential we saw in it that others didn't. For first home buyers, the compromise is a little different as their core objective should be getting a foot on the property ladder. This may mean not living in the property. So the size/quality dimension almost becomes a compulsory compromise and gets replaced with the desire to live at the property rather than rent it out. If they want to live at a property (they can commute to work from) they will need to compromise on location and quality/size. Alternatively they can keep the location, buy something smaller and not so nice and rent it out (think unloved studio instead of tidy two bedroom unit) or purchase

in a nice location within a more affordable area away from their local city centre and rent it out.

Most first home buyers aren't looking to become an investor, however many of them work in capital cities and often can't afford to buy where they want to live. With the right income you can compromise and buy a small unit in an expensive city like Sydney, but as at 2017 this will still set you back around $500,000. That's a $100,000 (20%) deposit if you want to avoid Lenders Mortgage Insurance (LMI). I will discuss this further on page 69.

So let's say you've managed to save $50,000 which, income allowing, would get you a budget of $250,000. That's unlikely to buy much in Sydney or Melbourne not

The core objective should be getting on the property ladder. This may mean not living in it

too far from the CBD. However, if you think about the purchase as an investment and rent where you want to live, then a one bedroom unit in Brisbane (or say Hamilton in New Zealand) becomes an option. As the rent helps pay the mortgage you build equity that can be used later. Capital gains are a bonus. Yes it's true that even if your investment in Brisbane increases in value, the place you really want in Sydney has too, but you're on the ladder. Often, in lower price brackets you'll find the rent covers most of the mortgage payments which means you may still have money left over to save.

Additionally, you can leverage your equity to purchase another investment property and accelerate your gains. Of course that assumes there are gains and no 'market correction' but if you are covering repayments with rent and in it for the long term (10+ years) history suggests you will be ok. Ten years is a long time, but if you start at 30 you'll have a good base to launch from when you're 40. You can also rent where you really want to live while you're young. Additionally, as at 2017 negative gearing is still available in Australia and while it has no doubt been a key reason as to why housing has become unaffordable, it doesn't mean you shouldn't take advantage of it if you qualify.

If at any point your income is a little higher and you've built some equity you can sell and use that as a deposit on the place you actually want to live in.

Property stats

Why they're important.

Property statistics can be seen as irrelevant to the general public, but are really important to understand before making an offer on a home. It's the biggest financial commitment you'll ever make. You want to do everything you can to pay the right price as anything extra is going straight onto the mortgage.

The best way to truly understand a property's value is through these stats.

AVM (AUTOMATED VALUATION MODEL): A computer generated estimate of a property's current value. The calculation takes into consideration a range of factors, but is significantly driven by 'For sale' and 'Sold' prices of comparable properties in the area. Banks use these when assessing your loan so they don't have to pay a valuer to physically inspect the property. However, unique properties still require a physical inspection. It is presented as an estimated figure and a 'confidence score' indicating how accurate the estimate is. A good estimate is within 10% of the true value.

COMPARABLES: Comparable properties aren't 'stats' but provide excellent real life examples similar to the one you're looking at. Comparables are usually the same size and location as the target property and have either recently sold or are currently for sale.

MEDIAN SALE PRICE: The median is simply the middle value of a data set (like the 50th percentile in a child's growth charts). It is often preferred to using an 'average' as it doesn't get skewed by particularly large or small values. When used in property it gives an indication of how much you'd expect to pay for a middle of the road property in a particular area. For example, if the median sale price in Sydney is $1 million you would expect half of the properties to be worth less than $1 million and half to be worth more. Median sale prices can be compared across suburbs or cities and over time to track price growth.

Median Sale Prices - September 2016

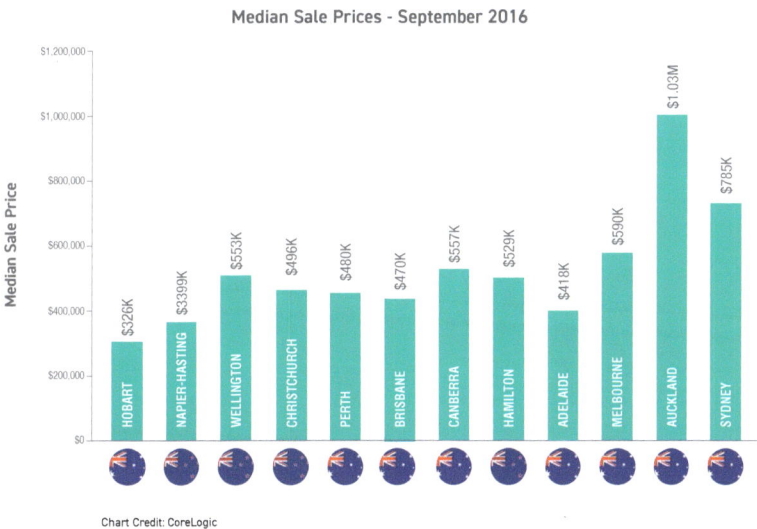

Chart Credit: CoreLogic

Note: If you're wondering why the median sale price for Sydney and Melbourne looks low it's because they have a much higher proportion of units than cities in New Zealand including Auckland. This brings the overall median sale price down as units are much more affordable than houses.

MEDIAN PRICE CHANGE: This is the change in the median value over a period of time, expressed as a percentage. The most commonly reported yearly changes are one, three and five and give an idea of the pace of growth in different markets. You can see below just how different the one year growth rates were across the different Australian and New Zealand cities in September 2016.

Median Price Change - September 2016

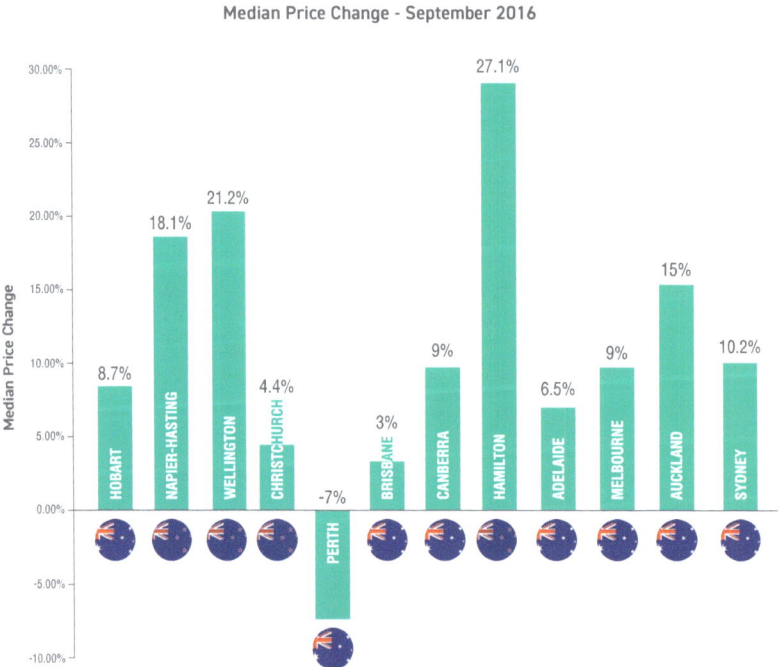

Chart Credit: CoreLogic

AVERAGE DAYS ON MARKET: This is the average time it takes to sell property in a particular area. It starts on the first listing date and ends on the date it is officially sold. In weaker markets properties take longer to sell placing more power in the buyer's hands, whereas the opposite occurs where the days on market is low. Typically 30 to 60 days is considered a healthy market, while it's not uncommon to see average days on market over 100.

AVERAGE VENDOR DISCOUNTING: This is the difference between the original asking price and the actual sale price of a property - effectively how much did the owner discount the property to make the sale? Vendor discounting and days on market are often linked as in slower markets they both increase and in stronger markets they decrease. As a buyer you are able to be more aggressive with your offers when the days on market and discounting levels for a suburb are high. Conversely, as a seller you can feel more confident rejecting offers when the days on market and discounting levels are low.

AUCTION RESULTS: Not so much a stat but a great way to keep an eye on real examples of market results. These are published on real estate listing portals and local newspapers following weekend auctions and include the sale price or whether the property was 'passed in' (not sold).

CLEARANCE RATES: These represent what proportion of auctions resulted in a sale. Strong markets will have higher clearance rates, in some cases up to 90% or more. Throughout periods of strong value growth cities in Australia and New Zealand have had clearance rates over 70%, which is considered healthy. We would expect to see clearance rates decline before seeing a downward shift in property values.

We would expect to see clearance rates decline before a downward shift in property values

GROSS YIELD: The yield is something investors are interested in as it represents the return they get from the property. It is simply the annual rent divided by the property value. With values outstripping rental growth the yield in Australia and New Zealand is close to an all time low (around 3%), although there are still markets where yield is much healthier (usually lower value regional areas).

STREET/SUBURB MIX: A number of websites will now show you the split of owners vs renters and houses vs units in a street or suburb. For example, you may want to favour locations which are predominantly owner occupied houses rather than rented units. Investors may favour the opposite.

OTHER THINGS TO CONSIDER: You can view all existing development applications (DA's) such as renovations or new builds in a street or suburb to get an idea of the investment people are making in the area. Similarly keep an eye out for council plans for upgraded infrastructure in the area.

The Census can get a bit outdated but it's also a useful tool for understanding the population change in a neighbourhood or city.

Suggested Resources:

Commbank Property Guide
commbank.com.au/personal/home-loans/commbank-property-app.html

CoreLogic.com.au

Domain.com.au

Qv.co.nz

Onthehouse.com.au

PropertyValue.com.au

RealEstate.com.au

Homes.co.nz

Buying

Classic factors to consider.

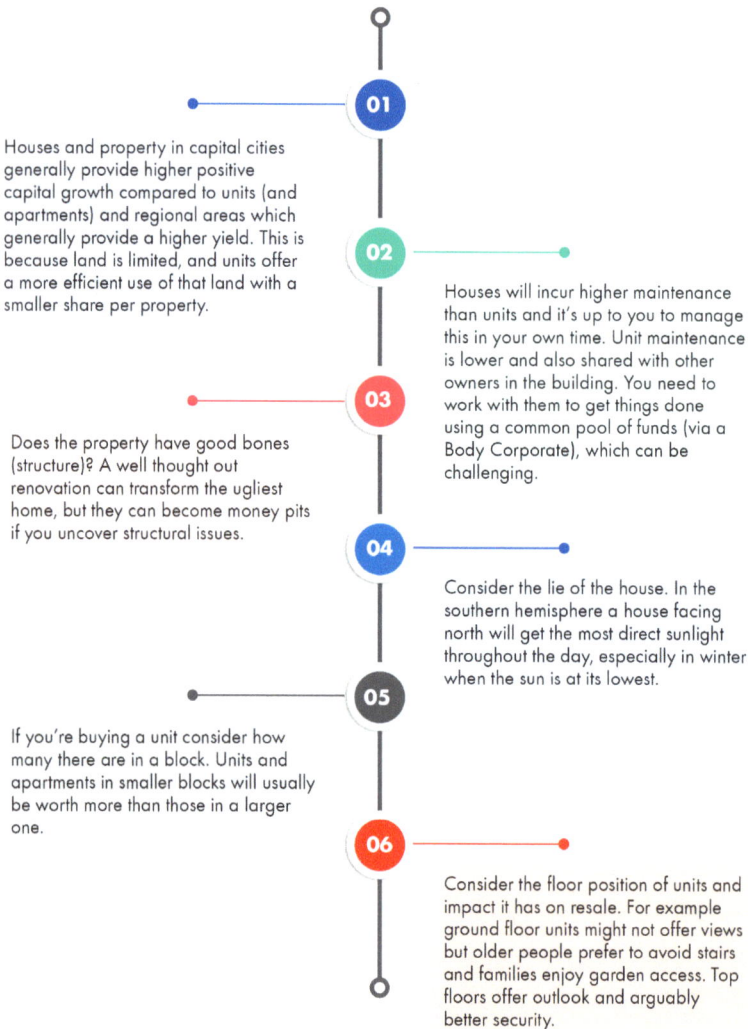

01

Houses and property in capital cities generally provide higher positive capital growth compared to units (and apartments) and regional areas which generally provide a higher yield. This is because land is limited, and units offer a more efficient use of that land with a smaller share per property.

02

Houses will incur higher maintenance than units and it's up to you to manage this in your own time. Unit maintenance is lower and also shared with other owners in the building. You need to work with them to get things done using a common pool of funds (via a Body Corporate), which can be challenging.

03

Does the property have good bones (structure)? A well thought out renovation can transform the ugliest home, but they can become money pits if you uncover structural issues.

04

Consider the lie of the house. In the southern hemisphere a house facing north will get the most direct sunlight throughout the day, especially in winter when the sun is at its lowest.

05

If you're buying a unit consider how many there are in a block. Units and apartments in smaller blocks will usually be worth more than those in a larger one.

06

Consider the floor position of units and impact it has on resale. For example ground floor units might not offer views but older people prefer to avoid stairs and families enjoy garden access. Top floors offer outlook and arguably better security.

School zones

A study[4] in New Zealand analysed over 10,000 house sales in a group of inner Auckland suburbs over 21 years. When a good school increased its boundary to include a new suburb, the house prices in this suburb began to attract a premium compared to relative suburbs (growing to NZ$66,000 over 10 years). When a suburb was relocated out of a school zone, this premium diminished.

A similar study[5] conducted by Redfin in U.S.A. looked at the median sale price and price per square foot of homes within school zones, comparing the test scores of schools across the country. They found home buyers paid $50 more per square foot for homes located within top ranked school districts. The study found nearly identical homes just a short distance apart could vary in price by as much as $130,000 because of the difference in school districts. So even if you don't have kids it's a good idea to check out the local schools. Just keep an eye out for future re-zoning!

Public Transport

As you'd expect, access to public transport also improves property value, but by how much? A study[6] commissioned by the American Public Transportation Association and the National Association of Realtors looked at sales data over five years in several major American cities with varying levels of public transport infrastructure. On average, values for properties located within a half mile of public transportation, performed 41% better than properties located outside that coveted area. Anecdotally on the Upper East Side of New York apartment values drop by up to 15% for every block you move away from the subway line.

4:https://www.researchgate.net/publication/247630895_The_impact_of_geographically_defined_school_zones_on_house_prices_in_New_Zealand

5:https://www.redfin.com/blog/2013/09/paying-more-for-a-house-with-a-top-public-school-its-elementary.html

6:http://www.bankrate.com/finance/real-estate/public-transportation-affects-home-values.spx#ixzz4MUfBO4v0

Thinking one step ahead

Picking the right spot.

Auckland experienced large growth between 2012 and 2017, to the point where some families have been completely priced out of the housing market. Many of those that managed to purchase moved further out from their inner city suburb rentals.

In 2014 we noticed quite a few Facebook friends were buying in and around Avondale in the western suburbs. Avondale wouldn't be classed as 'inner west' but is still reasonably central and not as far west as a suburb like Henderson.

It's also on the train line with great access into the city. After doing some research I found our friends weren't alone, and this migration of professional workers was driving prices up in that location.

Brady and I had been looking to buy another investment property at the time and Avondale didn't meet our budget. However, just one suburb further west along the train line was New Lynn which was significantly cheaper. New Lynn, like most western suburbs of Auckland, had generally been working class and not popular with younger city workers. However, it has a train line into the city, is just five minutes from Avondale and a great well known school (Kelston Boys High) is in zone. Importantly, some quick research uncovered a council plan to upgrade the business district. This involved creating mixed use, higher density neighbourhoods with parks anchored by transport and employment hubs. By 2030, New Lynn could be home to 20,000 people with another 14,000 working there. While this would take time, we were in it for the long haul and happy to wait.

We ended up buying a three bedroom bungalow in Koromiko Street for $520,000 and tidied it up for about $20,000 (fence, new cupboards, polished floorboards, bathroom touch up and lots of paint). While it's a rental it could equally have been our first home.

Three years later QV.co.nz and Homes.co.nz valued it at around $750,000. This represents $210,000 (39%) in growth. It's true that buying any property over that period in Auckland would see a value increase, but this above average growth rate suggests we've selected a suburb that was not only affordable, but is realising its potential more than others.

As at 2017 you are unlikely to buy a house in New Lynn for $520,000 given the 'bubble-like' growth pricing many families out. If I was starting from scratch again I would follow the same process and maybe look at a brick and tile ground floor unit further out west along the train line. A quick look shows me a few two bedroom units in Henderson for under $400,000. Alternatively, Hamilton and Tauranga (which are major centres in the North Island) are more affordable despite experiencing growth as part of the ripple effect from Auckland.

Further out (and somewhat of a left field choice), although the population, employment and property value growth doesn't stand out, I like the look of New Plymouth on the west coast of the central North Island which is doing some great things and prices are on a different level. I have also noticed a few friends moving back to country areas and commuting to Auckland (similar to colleagues here in Sydney), which may become more of a trend, especially as flexible working becomes more common with faster internet. None of these may suit your needs, but the point remains that you need to be one step ahead and compromise.

- Use the train line or other public transport routes to narrow your focus

- Use Facebook to monitor where people are moving. There's often a pattern (in Sydney's Northern Beaches many of our friends are moving further north where houses are bigger and cheaper than Manly)

- Keep an eye out for council infrastructure and revitalisation plans

- Think about future trends based on other countries. For example, apartment living is more popular in Sydney and Melbourne than it is in Auckland and I see more people compromising on size to continue living centrally. Just beware of apartment over supply in some areas

CHAPTER THREE
SELLING

Selecting an agent

Do your research.

An agent once told me I put him through his most rigorous selection process in 20 years. For many you're just another commission, but this is your largest asset and you want the best possible result.

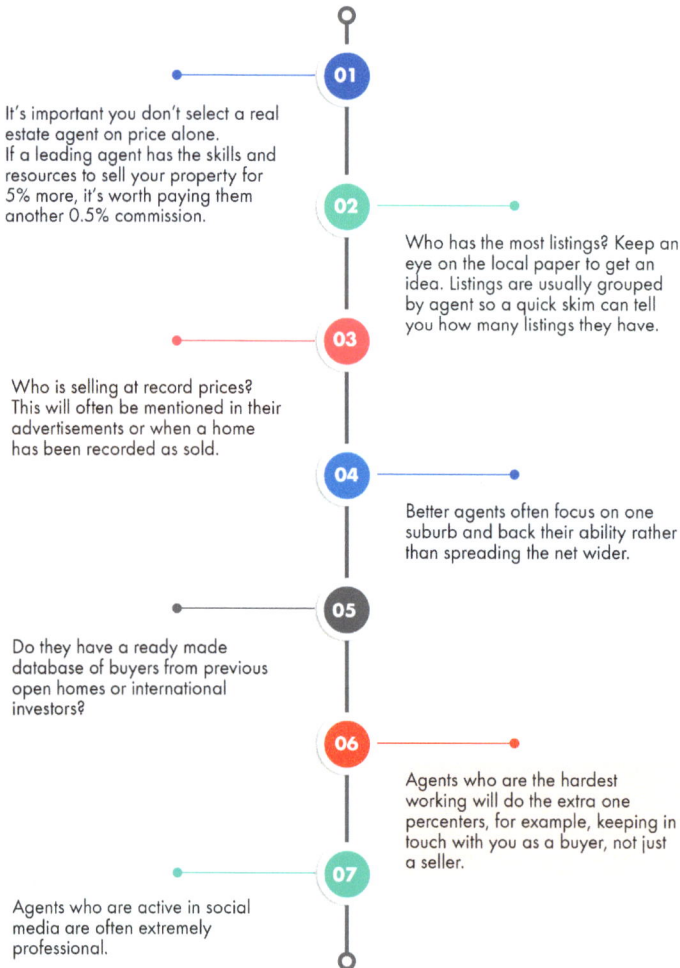

01

It's important you don't select a real estate agent on price alone.
If a leading agent has the skills and resources to sell your property for 5% more, it's worth paying them another 0.5% commission.

02

Who has the most listings? Keep an eye on the local paper to get an idea. Listings are usually grouped by agent so a quick skim can tell you how many listings they have.

03

Who is selling at record prices? This will often be mentioned in their advertisements or when a home has been recorded as sold.

04

Better agents often focus on one suburb and back their ability rather than spreading the net wider.

05

Do they have a ready made database of buyers from previous open homes or international investors?

06

Agents who are the hardest working will do the extra one percenters, for example, keeping in touch with you as a buyer, not just a seller.

07

Agents who are active in social media are often extremely professional.

Price and commissions

They need to work for everyone not just you.

The market will dictate what your property is worth, and definitely not how much you need to sell it for. The longer a property is on the market the more difficult it becomes to sell. This is what the industry refers to as a property going 'smelly' as people start wondering what's wrong with it.

You can get a really good idea of the property value using property stats like the AVM (a property's computer estimated value) and recent sales in the area.

Your agent will be using these same stats to provide you a market appraisal, in combination with their own market knowledge.

Agreeing on a price guide and sales commission with the real estate agent.

It's tempting to select the agent who provides you the highest appraisal of your home, and this is what many people do. In the past some agents have increased their estimated value to win the listing. They would then quote a much lower figure to interested buyers to widen the net and the actual sale price would fall between the two numbers.

There has been an increase in industry regulation on 'under' and 'over' quoting so that agents have to provide a written estimate of the property value which is no wider than 10% ($1 million - $1.1 million for example). This figure is shown to both the vendor and also interested buyers. It remains a guide only and the property can sell above or below this but it makes it illegal to quote one figure to the vendor ($1.2 million) and another to buyers ($900,000). Agents can be fined for consistently quoting inaccurate estimates so the best agencies will use a combination of property stats and multiple agent's opinions to come to their estimate.

We have had success using a tiered system when agreeing on a commission.

Rather than a flat rate regardless of the sale price, the agent gets paid a higher commission rate as the price increases and significantly less as it decreases.

The reason this works is that with a flat rate system another $25,000 on the sale price is great for you, but the agent will only get 2% of that extra amount - just $500! It is better for them to convince you to accept an early offer, sell and move on to their next listing, especially if it means avoiding another open home.

I find the best way to agree on different tiers is use the agent's price guide when initially winning your listing. For a price guide of $700,000 to $770,000 you might have a commission of 1.8% for a result under $700,000, right up to 2.5% for a result over $770,000. This will put them on the spot and help avoid inflated quoting.

SALE PRICE	COMMISSION RATE
Under $700,000	1.8%
$700,000 - $770,000	2.2%
More than $770,000	2.5%

- If the sale price is $700,000 they would get paid 2.2% of this which equals $15,400.

- If the sale price is $780,000 they would get paid 2.5% of this which equals $19,500 (27% more).

While the commission rate increases and keeps your agent motivated you still make more money so everyone wins.

Keep in mind that the higher the property value, the lower the commission percentage. The agent effectively does a similar amount of work for a property worth $700,000 or $1.4 million but gets close to double the commission on the $1.4 million property at the same commission percentage. As a rule of thumb, agents charge 2% plus GST (2.2%) in Australia and this can come down to mid 1%'s or lower for high value properties and particularly competitive markets.

What about flat fee models?

This is where the agent charges a flat fee to sell your home instead of charging commission. The arguments both for and against this model are the agent fee isn't tied to the sale price.

For example, in 2008 a company in New Zealand called The Joneses offered a flat fee model priced at $7,995 per sale. At the time the average commission was around $12,000 or more. They also paid their staff a flat salary regardless of the sale. Their argument was this allowed staff to focus on selling the home for the best price. The Joneses lasted just 18 months. The lower fee and guaranteed salaries for close to 80 staff put pressure on them to win listings and sell properties. As most people stayed with the system they knew and understood, this model wasn't accepted quickly enough to save the company.

Why didn't more people use them? I talk a little bit about 'getting what you pay for' on page 92 and while I'm not suggesting The Joneses offered a poor service I personally want the very best handling my biggest asset. That might seem obvious, but the best agents are unlikely to move to an 'everyone gets a similar salary' model. This is probably where some readers will disagree with me as I believe higher performers and those in highly impactful roles (such as a CEO) should be paid a lot more than others.

That being said, the flat fee model is still out there. In Australia 'Purplebricks' have offered a $4,500 flat fee which appears to include photography and online advertising. So if you remain convinced, then go for it!

Selling methods

Private Treaty vs Auction.

Regardless of how the agent is remunerated you still need to agree on a sale method with them. The most popular methods in Australia and New Zealand are Private Treaty and Auction.

Private Treaty

This is probably the most straightforward method of sale in that the vendor sets an asking price and negotiates with prospective buyers (via the agent).

A contract of sale determines the official offer and this can be conditional, meaning certain items such as a satisfactory building inspection or approved finance need to occur for the contract to be valid. The asking price needs to identify realistic buyers so it's particularly important to make sure it isn't too high to scare away buyers or too low to reduce the final sale price.

As the sale campaign typically takes 4-6 weeks, offers can be made throughout this period. Both parties have time to consider offers and the vendor is able to amend the asking price based on market feedback.

40

Auction

This is arguably more stressful for both buyers and sellers because all offers occur at the same time at a specific place (although pre-auction offers can be considered).

An auctioneer, who manages the auction, asks for an opening bid somewhere around the guide price with buyers calling out bids increasing in value. The property is 'selling' when it reaches the vendor's reserve (the lowest amount they are willing to sell for) and from there the highest bidder wins the auction.

They then need to immediately pay a 10% deposit to secure the property. If the reserve isn't met the property is passed in to the highest bidder, who has exclusive rights to negotiate with the vendor for a period of time.

Auctions can be good for vendors as they create a sense of urgency and directly pit emotional buyers against each other. They can also consider 'pre-auction offers' and sell before the auction day. Unlike a private treaty where offers are confidential, the transparency of the process is great for buyers as they can see how many bidders there are and what they are willing to pay.

One possible downside for vendors is pressure to lower the future asking price if the property is passed in (not sold at auction). A negative for buyers is there is no cooling off period so all bids are final and not subject to any conditions that haven't already been agreed with the vendor.

Consider a property staging company. They have interior designers who will put together a plan for your home and provide required furniture

Preparing your home for sale

How to maximise your sale price.

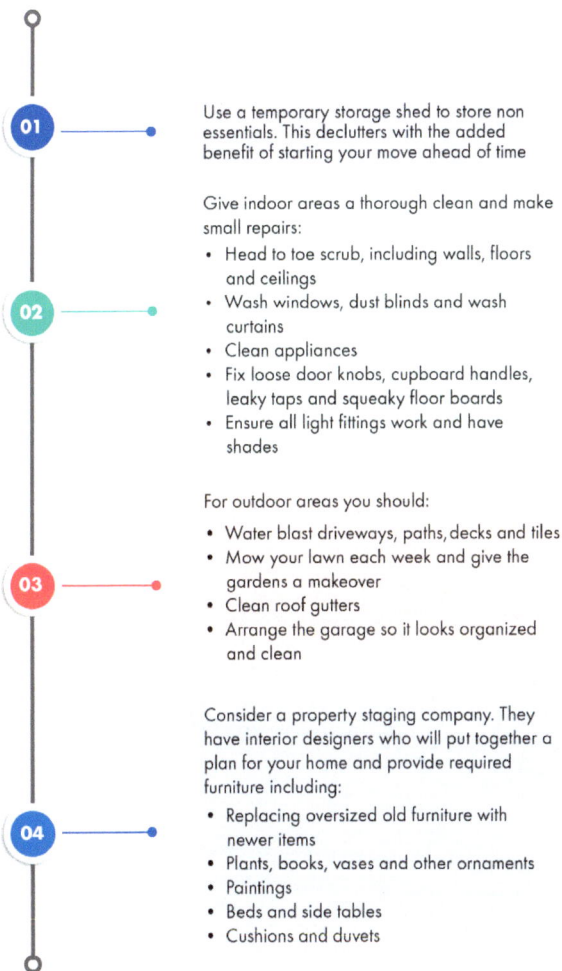

01 — Use a temporary storage shed to store non essentials. This declutters with the added benefit of starting your move ahead of time

02 — Give indoor areas a thorough clean and make small repairs:
- Head to toe scrub, including walls, floors and ceilings
- Wash windows, dust blinds and wash curtains
- Clean appliances
- Fix loose door knobs, cupboard handles, leaky taps and squeaky floor boards
- Ensure all light fittings work and have shades

03 — For outdoor areas you should:
- Water blast driveways, paths, decks and tiles
- Mow your lawn each week and give the gardens a makeover
- Clean roof gutters
- Arrange the garage so it looks organized and clean

04 — Consider a property staging company. They have interior designers who will put together a plan for your home and provide required furniture including:
- Replacing oversized old furniture with newer items
- Plants, books, vases and other ornaments
- Paintings
- Beds and side tables
- Cushions and duvets

Don't get carried away by large numbers of open home visitors. There are alot of nosy neighbours

Offers and settlement

A bird in the hand is worth two in the bush.

Tyre kickers

When we sold our unit in Manly we had over 100 groups through. There was literally a line out the door and around the building on the first day. We even got a very healthy offer early the next week which we declined as we wanted to see what else would come through.

Despite the massive traffic we only had 10 groups who requested a contract. From those 10 about half came back two or three times but by the third week we hadn't received another offer. Based on this our agent went back to the original buyer and suggested the auction could be avoided if he increased the offer slightly. He did and we took it. The point here is that offers are like gold, no matter how low and you shouldn't get carried away with large numbers coming to your open home (many of which will be nosy neighbours anyway).

Settlement

Once the property is sold you enter the 'settlement period' which is usually around six weeks but can be as short or as long as you like - although it needs to be agreed with the buyer presale. This allows time for lawyers to process everything and make sure any costs are fairly split (right down to each party paying a proportional share of council rates) and for the banks to process funds. It also gives both parties time to prepare their respective moves.

CHAPTER FOUR
RENOVATING

Renovating appropriately

Getting the balance right.

Brady and I love renovating as we can add our own mark to the property and create value. We have done a couple of renovations and are in the process of building our new home. Each of them has been very different.

MAINTAIN IT.

Clonbern Road is a beautiful old villa in Remuera, Auckland that we purchased as our first home and have rented since 2008. While dated inside, everything is in good condition so we have taken a 'proactive maintenance' approach to this property as it is in a nice area. A new roof, fence, path and gates have been the main investments with ongoing fixes being managed by our Property Manager. There will come a time where we take a 'full renovation' approach.

UPDATE IT.

Koromiko Street is a classic three bedroom weatherboard house in New Lynn, Auckland. We bought it as an investment and the renovation was to bring it up to speed in a cost effective manner. We could have rented it 'as is', but felt that with a tidy up we could command another $50 a week and get our investment back over the coming years. We ripped up the carpet, polished the floorboards, painted the kitchen cupboards and added new handles. A new toilet and vanity and a lick of paint throughout was enough. We also fixed the fence and gave it a coat of white paint. The entire renovation cost about $20,000 immediately after purchasing the property for $520,000.

GUT IT.

Stuart Street was a 1970s brown brick unit in Manly, Sydney. People tried their best to say something nice but we knew what they were thinking, especially when they saw the lime green feature wall. This renovation was mainly cosmetic, with the exception of two walls being removed. We gutted the whole thing, opened up the kitchen which had an internal laundry and knocked down the wall between two sliding doors out to the balcony creating stacker doors across the entire lounge. Floating floors created consistency and space throughout. The kitchen, bathroom and ensuite were upgraded, all with high-end appliances to meet the needs of a family of five in a premium location. We completed the look with paint throughout, new tiling on the balcony as well as introducing a heap of shelving in the garage to maximise storage space. We were lucky the balcony balustrades were rotten so the strata paid to replace these (as they were deemed common property). We paid $830,000 for the unit and spent about $120,000 on the renovation. Four years later we sold it for $1.62 million, also helped by the rapidly rising property market.

DETONATE IT.

Hill Street, our forever home. As I write this we are waiting for our development approval to come through in Queenscliff, Sydney, for an old brick cottage which is more cost effective to demolish than renovate. This will leave us with a good sized block of land with ocean views. It's been a long process working with the architect while also looping in builders to make sure we keep our designs within a reasonable budget. Early communication with different professionals is something I have found to be really helpful. The builder has been able to offer advice and also provide rough costings throughout, allowing us to scale back where needed. We are also working with our broker on the construction loan application to make sure there are no surprises and the accountant has also answered questions about how the costs can be best managed from a tax perspective.

So your renovation very much needs to be 'fit for purpose' and the first thing you need to determine is your objective:

- **Are you renovating for profit?**
- **Are you renovating your dream home?**
- **Are you simply making it liveable?**
- **Or maybe general maintenance and improvement?**

Overcapitalising

Renovating almost always adds value to the property (at a cost), but there is a limit to the value you can add and this is largely determined by property values in the suburb. Overcapitalising is when the cost of renovations outweighs the value it adds to the property, so you actually put more in than you get back. A useful approach to avoid this is by understanding the prices of both unrenovated and renovated properties in the suburb. This way you can estimate the value after renovation and determine your budget.

For example:

> **Average purchase price of unrenovated properties of a similar size and location to yours = $650,000**
>
> **Average purchase price of renovated properties of a similar size and location to yours = $800,000**

So the maximum renovation budget should be less than $150,000 (~25% of the property value), but ideally a lot less to give yourself wiggle room and potentially increase your equity. The percentage you spend is dependent on your objective. For example you can justify spending more on your dream home, but less on making something liveable. This can be a real balancing act, especially when looking to make a profit as cutting the budget too much will limit the value you can add and make it more difficult to sell to people who want to buy something which is ready to live in.

Cosmetic changes such as painting, flooring, kitchens and bathrooms are generally more affordable than structural changes such as extending or adding a level so this will impact the budget too.

Of course, people also renovate for pure lifestyle reasons (for example, a pool or a deck) and that's fine too as long as you do it knowing it comes at a cost you may not recover.

Also don't forget to check whether you need council approval and understand any potential fees they might hit you with.

How much to spend?

A general rule of thumb is a budget of between 5% and 10% of the current property value. This will increase in higher value locations and where the gap between unrenovated and renovated properties is larger or if you plan to live in the property for a long time.

Using our personal examples we spent:

- 4% of the property value (and purchase price) for Clonbern Road. We have spent about $50,000 over ten years with the property currently worth about $1.3 million (purchase price $570,000)

- 4% of the property value (and purchase price) for Koromiko Street

- 13% of the value for Stuart Street (purchased for $830,000 but worth about $920,000 when we started the renovation)

- Hill Street is quite different as we paid $2.2 million plus stamp duty for the property and the new build will cost us another $1.2 million (55% of the property value). However the property value is all in the land, so the ability to add value via building is much higher.

  Renovated properties in the street sold for between $3.5 million and $5 million in 2017 and the bank has provided a post build value of $3.7 million so we're confident we aren't overcapitalising (although the mortgage still has to be paid)

Which areas of a property should I renovate?

While setting a budget you'll be identifying the areas most in need of work and those most likely to add value. This will help allocate the budget to different areas of the property. When doing this you need to be realistic about how far the budget will stretch and add a margin for error of at least 10%, but ideally 20% extra. It's a cliche to say every property is different, but it's true. Only you will know the hidden opportunities for renovation. However, there are areas of a house that consistently have the biggest impact.

- Kitchens and bathrooms generally add the most value, although they cost more. A basic kitchen is going to set you back at least $10,000 but larger kitchens fitted out to higher specifications will cost $20,000 to $40,000 and the sky is the limit after that. Standard bathrooms are around $5,000 with higher end renovations starting at around $10,000 and going up to $20,000 or more. If I'm looking to add value I generally start with these two items first

- Open plan living is key, ideally with a seamless flow to outdoor areas. Knocking out walls to open up space and light combined with bifold or stacker doors out to a deck, balcony or garden provides indoor/outdoor flow and a great breeze way. Outdoor living is highly valued in Australia and New Zealand, so try to create a usable outside space for entertaining and children's play. Fencing, decking, landscaping and off street parking are all great ways to improve not just the value of your home, but general liveability

- With unit and apartment living becoming more common, space is becoming a premium. When we removed the laundry space from the kitchen area at Stuart Street we stacked the washer/dryer in a cupboard. Just make sure you get a condenser dryer. We also added built-in wardrobes and storage cupboards plus shelving in the garage

- There are plenty of small, low cost improvements that can really add up. Smaller items we have found make an impact are polished floors, new paint, cupboard and door handles and light fittings. There are also cost effective ways to heat and cool a property which are highly valued by tenants and buyers

- It's difficult to place a value on something you can't see. While plumbing and wiring can add great cost to your renovation, they do not add much financial value. I say 'financial value' because these hidden improvements are not only necessities, they improve the comfort and safety of the home. A lot of the time these items are unavoidable but you can still consider their impact in your renovation plans. For example, moving the kitchen to another location will likely involve moving the existing plumbing which will add further costs. Or if you're about to sell and the roof is getting a bit old you might be better keeping your money in your pocket and leaving it as is

- There aren't too many features that can have a negative return, but swimming pools are an example as some buyers don't want to bother with the maintenance, or feel they are too dangerous for young children. If the pool is for your family to enjoy for a long time then go for it, but maybe don't look at it as a key way to add value

Smaller items that make an impact are polished floors, new paint, cupboard and door handles and light fittings

Based on this you might allocate 25% to the kitchen, 20% to the bathroom(s), 20% to the exterior and outdoor areas, leaving 35% for other improvements. In the previous example of the property being worth $650,000 with renovated properties selling for $800,000 we could work with a 10% budget of $65,000 and allocate as follows:

- $15,000 kitchen

- $10,000 bathroom(s)

- $15,000 bifolds
  (may require some engineering if the wall is load bearing)

- $10,000 for a simple deck out from the bifolds

- $10,000 floating floorboards (or polish the existing ones)

- $5,000 internal paint

Allowing a 20% margin of error, the likely total cost is about $80,000. These figures assume a basic to middle end finish for a small to medium house. This would bring the total investment to about $730,000 which still leaves some wiggle room under $800,000 if you intend to sell.

If you're looking for inspiration it's worth buying a few house design magazines and signing up to Pinterest. My wife often creates a scrap book which helps document what we like.

Finally, even if you're renovating your dream home it's worthwhile doing your best to keep things neutral in case you ever do need to sell. This will help the property appeal to a wider range of buyers. If you're simply looking to make money you need to take this even further and completely remove the emotion from your choices. While you might think those gold taps and chandelier look great in the bathroom others may not like them enough to pay the premium you did for them.

CHAPTER FIVE
FINANCE

Mortgage interest rates

To fix or float?

Should you lock in a fixed interest rate or roll the dice on a variable (floating) rate? Does anyone really know? The answer is no. However, you can improve your chance of making a good decision by understanding how each type of mortgage works.

A key difference is variable mortgage rates depend on where interest rates are today while fixed rates depend on what the market is expecting interest rates to average in the future. To provide fixed rate mortgages, lenders access funds with relatively fixed costs over longer terms. Another difference is that fixed interest rates provide certainty which you don't get with a variable rate and are for an agreed loan term - generally between one and five years in Australia and New Zealand, with the most popular historically being three. Throughout this period the rate will not change and you know in advance what your repayments will be. This makes it easier to budget and if rates rise, your repayments stay the same. However, you don't benefit from any fall in interest rates (unlike variable), as you are locked in until the end of your term. I remember working at Commonwealth Bank just after the Global Financial Crisis in 2008 when variable rates came crashing down from 9% to 6%. Customers calling in to switch their fixed rates (which were at 8% - 9%) were being told it would cost tens of thousands of dollars to break their agreement as the banks had funded those loans at higher rates.

Fixed loans are also less flexible; you can't make as many extra repayments and it's also more difficult to switch mortgage providers. I remember our bank no longer approving our home loan top up for a renovation when I became self-employed. We couldn't easily move to another bank to get the money because of our fixed rate loan.

Historically the variable mortgage rate has averaged around 7% in Australia and New Zealand, so that's a good guide to use when considering which way to go.

Of course variable rates have been well over 10% and below 4% in the past 30 years so you need to take current market factors into consideration too.

A split rate mortgage is where you hedge your bets and have part of your loan fixed and part variable.

This also means you can link an offset account to the variable rate component of your loan (more about this soon). Coming from New Zealand where most people traditionally fix their mortgage it took a bit of getting used to having a variable rate mortgage but it has worked well for us so far.

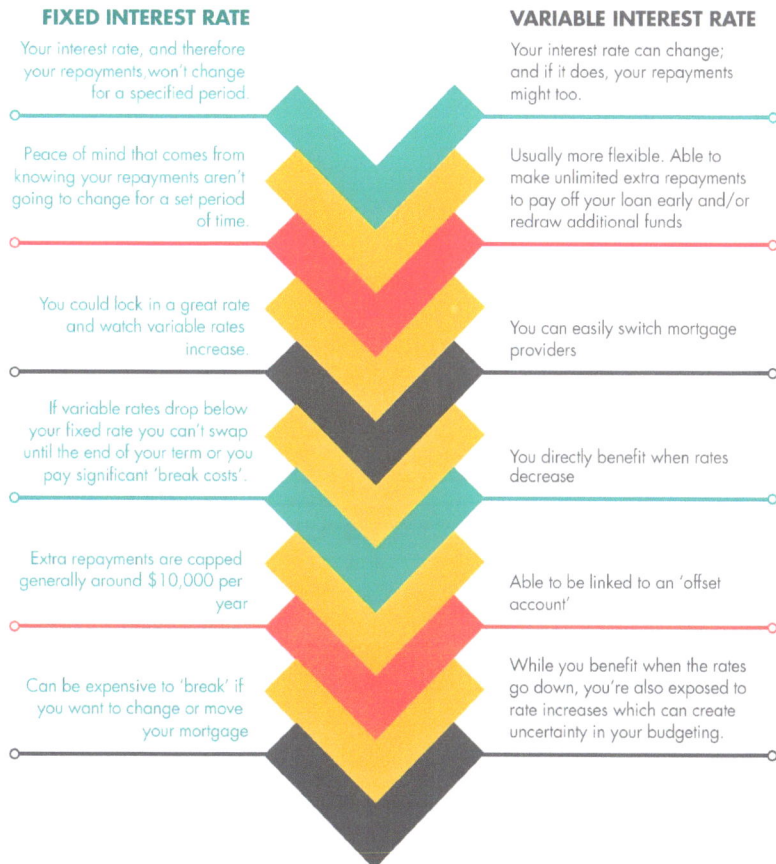

FIXED INTEREST RATE

Your interest rate, and therefore your repayments, won't change for a specified period.

Peace of mind that comes from knowing your repayments aren't going to change for a set period of time.

You could lock in a great rate and watch variable rates increase.

If variable rates drop below your fixed rate you can't swap until the end of your term or you pay significant 'break costs'.

Extra repayments are capped generally around $10,000 per year

Can be expensive to 'break' if you want to change or move your mortgage

VARIABLE INTEREST RATE

Your interest rate can change; and if it does, your repayments might too.

Usually more flexible. Able to make unlimited extra repayments to pay off your loan early and/or redraw additional funds

You can easily switch mortgage providers

You directly benefit when rates decrease

Able to be linked to an 'offset account'

While you benefit when the rates go down, you're also exposed to rate increases which can create uncertainty in your budgeting.

I have friends that pay 'interest only'. How does that work?

There are two components to a loan - the principal (which is the original amount you borrow) and the interest (the cost of borrowing the money). An interest only loan has lower repayments as you are only repaying the interest portion to stop the loan size from increasing. These loans are very popular with investors (around two in three investor loans are interest only) as they are often after capital gains and tax breaks with as little outlay as possible.

While traditionally not popular with owner occupiers, there has been an increase towards this type of loan in Australia with one in four owner occupier loans being interest only in 2016. This arguably, has been another factor in the 'bubble like' growth over the preceding period.

Interest only mortgages aren't necessarily a good idea for home owners because the lower the loan amount (the principal) you repay, the more you end up paying in interest. Unlike investors in

Australia, owner occupiers can't claim the interest against their taxable income. I believe the growing popularity of interest only loans was driven by a booming property market and people stretching themselves to the limit financially to get into it. Interest only might lower the repayments, but banks will generally only allow you to do this for up to five years at which point you'll need to pay the principal back too.

In summary, if you're an investor with a good amount of equity in your portfolio, interest only helps manage your cash flow and maximise your tax breaks. If you're an owner occupier I would only consider this as an emergency or temporary solution (maybe while one of you is on maternity leave before going back to work or you are renovating or building and need to temporarily manage cash flow). Don't rely on it as a way to be able to afford to buy the property in the first place. Ultimately you want to pay the mortgage back as quickly as possible, so plan for the worst and hope for the best.

Why is our interest rate different to our friends?

When you repay a $600,000 loan at 5% interest your total repayments over 30 years are just under $1.16 million. That's $560,000 ($18,667 per year) in margin, but the bank doesn't get all of that. They borrowed the initial $600,000 and have to pay interest on that loan. As most people repay the loan earlier than the full 30 year term and/or switch providers for a better rate they don't usually get the full 30 years benefit from you. So how much do the banks make and how does that impact the interest rate they offer you?

- The first thing is the 'net interest rate' margin, which tends to be 2% to 2.5% of your mortgage (this has trended down significantly since 2000) and placed on top of the 'cost of funds'. This is how much it costs them to source the money for you. The cost of funds plus the margin equals the interest rate you pay before any discounts are applied. There are usually a host of additional fees they will slap you with, but these are relatively minor. Note, they still need to take all their costs (staff, technology, branch costs etc.) out of this margin plus any discount they offer you
- The second factor is your 'LVR' (Loan to Value Ratio). This is the proportion of the property you will be paying for without the help of the bank (see page 68 for more info about LVR's). A lower LVR generally means a lower interest rate as there is less risk to the bank
- Loan size is also a contributor as larger loans generally justify a larger interest rate discount given they make the bank more money
- Another contributing factor the bank considers is how easy it is to sell the property if they need to (e.g. is it a nice house in a popular suburb or a unique property in a potentially volatile area, like a mining town)

This means those in an expensive house in a good area who have a large deposit will usually get a lower interest rate than someone buying a cheaper house with a small deposit. Not fair for first home buyers, but the banks need to manage their risk.

Don't rely on interest only payments as a way to afford the property in the first place

What if interest rates increase?

Rapidly rising interest rates are every home owners nightmare and they represent a genuine risk when taking on a mortgage. 7% - 8% is about the average rate paid over the last 30 years in Australia (tipping over 15% in the 1980s). As at 2017, interest rates are closer to 4% so it would be unwise to assume they will go much lower or stay as they are for the long term.

Why did they get so high in the 1980s? A key reason was that since 1993 the RBA (Reserve Bank of Australia) has targeted inflation at between 2 to 3 percent but in the 20 years up to the early 1990s, the average annual inflation rate was 9.2 per cent[7]. Keeping inflation in this range balances the chances of recession and unaffordable interest rates and manages the value of the Australian dollar. It's a massive juggling act but this tool is in place to lower the likelihood of it happening again (with no guarantees).

We might not hit rates of more than 10% in Australia and New Zealand in the next 5 (or even 20) years but it's a very real possibility rates will move from 4% to 6% or even closer to 8%. While I think lower rates are here for a while I'd recommend factoring in at least a 2% rise to any interest rate you sign up for to allow some comfortable wiggle room. If you cant afford that I'd recommend lowering your budget or creating a back up plan.

Historical Standard Variable Home Loan
Interest Rates Last 30 Years - Australia

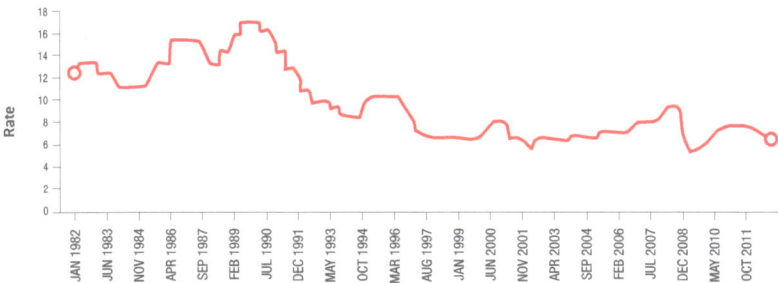

Chart credit: Loansense.com.au

7: http://www.marketeconomics.com.au/2435-keating-and-the-recession-we-had-to-have

Compounding interest

The key to managing your mortgage.

This is probably the biggest contributor to managing your mortgage as compounding interest can work both for and against you.

Let's take five coffees a week at $4 each and put that $80 as an extra monthly repayment on a $600,000 mortgage (5% interest). This saves $35,000 in interest and pays the loan off 18 months quicker. How? Well the $20 per week does two things:

1. Reduces the balance of your mortgage

2. Reduces the amount of interest that's added to your mortgage balance each month because the loan balance is lower

So not only is there an extra $80 a month coming off your mortgage, the monthly interest that's added is also reduced. My favourite way of making extra repayments without really noticing is to make fortnightly (or even weekly) rather than monthly repayments.

The following example is a $600,000 loan with a 5% interest rate. Monthly repayments over 30 years are $3,221. If we choose to pay half of that each fortnight ($1,611) we save $102,984 in interest and pay the loan off almost five years quicker. The main reason for this is the extra two fortnightly repayments you make over 52 weeks, meaning an extra $3,200 in repayments each year. You can also access the extra repayments you have made at a later date should you need them.

Fortnightly repayments can save you $100,000 in interest over the life of the loan

Fortnightly Vs Monthly Repayments at 5% Interest

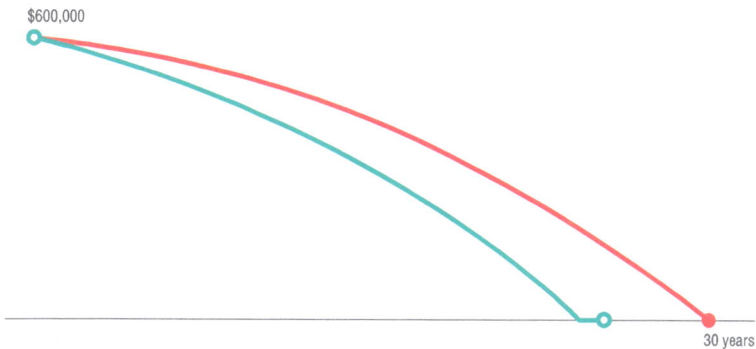

$600,000

30 years

By making fortnightly repayments, you could save up to $102.964 in interest and pay off your loan in 25 years and 4 months

Chart credit: Commbank.com.au

An offset account reduces the interest calculated on your loan

Offset accounts

Just 54%[8] of Australians definitely know what an offset account is. This is essentially a transactional account linked to your mortgage. Any money in the transaction account is 'offset' against your mortgage balance.

Mortgage balance: $600,000 @ 5% = $2,500 in interest per month

Offset account balance: $4,000

Interest payable calculated on balance of $596,000 = $2,484 = $16 savings per month

An offset account provides the same benefits as making extra repayments because any extra money in the account is included. If you're careful with your money you can keep your spare cash in the offset and still get the same benefits as making extra repayments. For me though, I find when there is extra money in my account I spend more. So I prefer a dual approach of fortnightly repayments which can't be missed and the offset account. You can always withdraw any extra repayments you've made.

01 Reduces the interest calculated on your loan based on the balance of your offset account

02 Keeps all your mortgage and savings in one place

03 Allows you access to your savings at any time, including via a debit card

04 Doesn't earn any interest on the savings, however you're saving interest on your mortgage and don't pay any tax on earnings (as there aren't any)

05 Some banks allow you to have more than one offset account so set all of your transaction accounts up to be offset against your mortgage (we have five offset accounts)

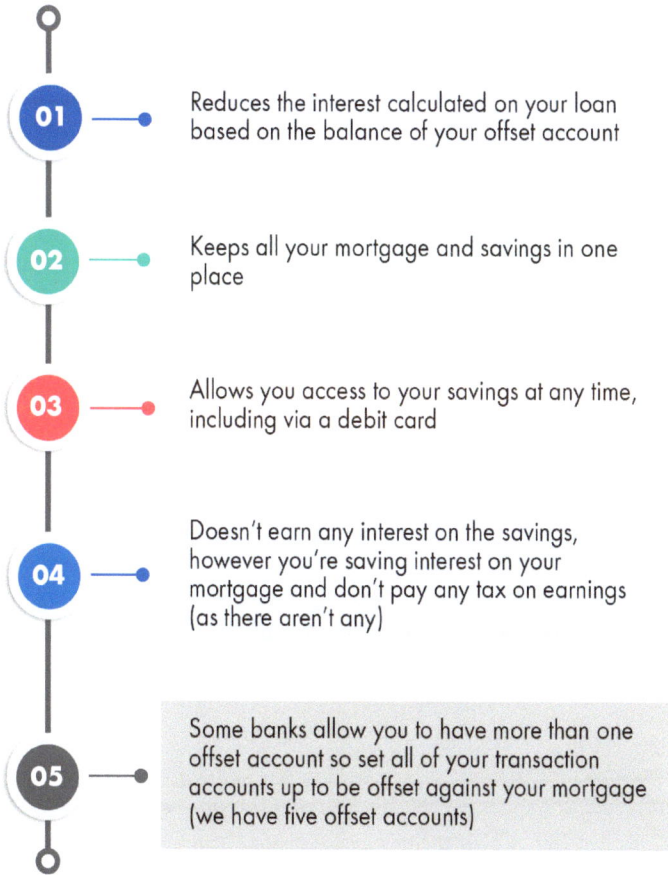

8: National study of 355 individuals who are currently paying off a home loan either as an owner occupier, (n=324), investor (n=59), or both (n=28). Study onducted by McCrindle from 9th-13th October 2015. http://mccrindle.com.au/blog/2015/12/Gateway%20CU%20A5%20 Infographic%20-%20digital.pdf

Loan to value ratios

How banks lower their risk on lending.

A n LVR (Loan to Value Ratio) is important as it restricts the amount a bank is willing to lend you. It's a way of calculating what proportion of the house you will be paying for up front without the help of the bank.

Banks are generally happy with an LVR up to 80% (a 20% deposit). This means if things go pear shaped and you miss your repayments, they can sell the property for 80% of its value and still get their mortgage back (leaving you with nothing). Additionally, to provide an extra buffer the bank's valuer will often price the property at the lower to middle end of its likely value. While this can be annoying as it restricts how much the bank will lend I find it's a good double check on how much you're offering to pay for the property.

> **LVR = total borrowings divided by the property value**
> **For example: $300,000/$500,000 = 60% LVR**

You've probably heard of 'mortgagee auctions'. These are effectively a 'fire sale' of someone's home with a very low reserve (or no reserve at all). Let's say in the example of the property with a $300,000 mortgage that it sells for $400,000.

As the bank has first rights to any sale proceeds they take the first $300,000 leaving you with $100,000 less any costs of sale (agent fees etc.). If the property sells for $280,000 the bank takes all of the money, leaving you with nothing AND they will come after you for the other $20,000 you owe them. This is different to America during the 2008 Global Financial Crisis where home owners could literally hand the keys back to the bank and walk away from the debt.

I've been told I don't need a 20% deposit to buy a home

With interest rates reaching record lows the main barrier for first home buyers is acquiring the initial deposit. Unfortunately, higher house prices mean a higher deposit is required to meet the 80% LVR. So for a $500,000 property you need $100,000 cash ready to put down before the bank will give you the mortgage. This also excludes any stamp duty you may have to pay in Australia. The first deposit is the hardest as future purchases can be funded with your 'equity' (more about equity soon).

There is one way around an 80% LVR, and it's called Lenders Mortgage Insurance (LMI) which is available in both Australia and New Zealand. With LMI the bank will lend you 90% to 95% of the property value. Sounds great right?

The big catch with LMI is that it's an insurance premium which covers the bank if you fail to make your repayments, so in the example of the fire sale where they were still $20,000 short of recovering what they initially lent you, the bank would be paid that shortfall by the insurance company. LMI does not cover you (that's why they call it Lenders Mortgage Insurance). So you're still left out of pocket if things go pear shaped AND you've paid the insurance premiums to cover the bank.

LMI isn't cheap either. If you wanted to borrow $450,000 instead of $400,000 for a $500,000 purchase, the LMI will set you back around $8,000. You can add that on top of your mortgage (making it $458,000) but you'll then pay interest on that $8,000 for 30 years and it will ultimately cost you more. That may still be worth it if you can get your home a couple of years sooner (when by that time the $500,000 property might be worth $516,000 anyway) so it's really something you need to weigh up against your personal views and situation.

Brokers

Why a good one is worth their weight in gold.

Mortgage broking first gained momentum in Australia in the early 1990s, representing 25% of the market by 2003. This rose to more than 50% of mortgages by 2015.

A mortgage broker is a go between, negotiating a mortgage with the bank on your behalf. They will pick up a lot of the paperwork and generally support you throughout the process. There is no charge for this service as the broker is paid a commission by the bank when the mortgage is settled (unlike bank lenders who are salaried). As they are only paid for sales this arguably makes brokers hungrier and more motivated to provide a good service to their customers. However, it can mean some brokers are 'pushy' and in some extreme cases negligent or reckless in an effort to get an application approved.

The commission payment comes in two components, an 'upfront' payment and a 'trail' (trailing commission). The upfront payment is about 0.6% of the mortgage size while the trail is about 0.15% of the mortgage each year for up to five years while the mortgage remains in place. So a $600,000 mortgage that stays with the same bank for five years would make a broker just over $8,000.

> **Up front: $600,000 x 0.60% = $3,600**
> **Trail: $600,000 x 0.15% x 5 = $4,500**
> **Total over 5 years = $8,100**

From the bank's perspective the $3,600 is similar to the marketing cost of acquiring a new mortgage while the 0.15% trail reflects a manageable portion of their margin.

There has been talk[9] of reviewing how the mortgage broking industry is paid, even looking at removing commission payments, but as at 2017 it is business as usual.

9:http://www.afr.com/brand/chanticleer/mortgage-broker-salad-days-are-numbered-20160525-gp3se5

"We're independent, so we are not biased"

01

Some mortgage brokers are actually owned by the same banks they bring customers to. An example is Commonwealth Bank who has a stake in Aussie Home Loans.

"We have the entire market to choose from, not just one bank's products."

02

Mortgage brokers do not necessarily select from the entire market, although with the market constantly changing this would be a very difficult thing to do. Aussie Home Loans, for example, select from thousands of mortgages so the selection is certainly wide.

"We'll get you the best deal and the loan that's right for you."

03

Legally, mortgage brokers have no obligation to find you the best or most suitable mortgage. Additionally, banks will have different offers or bonuses at any given time so it can be difficult to claim complete impartiality. However, it's also in their interest to find you the most suitable mortgage as they understand that a happy customer represents potential repeat business and referrals.

"Our service is free."

04

Yes, the service is free to you but remember they are well paid by the bank (who you pay) upon the mortgage being settled so remember that in your dealings with them.

A good broker can get you a better rate than you going direct to the bank

I have dealt both directly with the bank and via a mortgage broker and I wouldn't hesitate to go with a broker for all my lending going forward.

However, like most things in life it's all about the person. I was lucky enough to work with a very smart broker who offered an amazing service based on his hunger to earn his commission but also to be professional. He's with a smaller boutique company but came via a recommendation. If you don't have someone else's experience to go by I'd suggest going with a larger (national) mortgage broker to reduce the risk of getting a sub standard broker that isn't under the spotlight.

Finally, while you should let the broker do as much heavy lifting as possible make sure you do your own homework too. Simple things like keeping an eye on the current interest rates can help you have an intelligent conversation and keep them on their toes.

Refinancing

Make the banks work for your business.

Buying your home and moving in is really just the beginning because the mortgage is with you for the next 30 years - unfortunately a lot longer than the average marriage lasts. So it's in your best interest to stay informed about the mortgage market, especially when it's competitive. Yet 57% of Aussies don't know their current home loan rate[10].

It's rare for anyone to be paying 'price book' or the 'listed rate' on a mortgage these days, but there is still a wide variation in the level of discount given. As a general rule you should be receiving between 50 to 100 basis points discount (0.5% to 1%) and more for bigger loans with smaller LVR's (Loan to Value Ratio). To make sure you are receiving at least this discount, check the current variable interest rate of your bank against your mortgage.

You may have wondered why there are always two interest rates shown in a mortgage advertisement. The second, or 'comparison rate' is shown to help you see how different interest rates are comparable by factoring in upfront, ongoing and exit fees on mortgages. It also considers what the mortgage reverts to if there is a honeymoon rate (special rate for an initial period) or a Fixed Rate Mortgage and displays these costs as a combined interest rate.

10: RFi Group, September 2016, Do you know the interest rate that you're currently paying on your most recent loan? Base: Mortgage holders (n): 2,011.

I now prefer to negotiate a better rate via a broker rather than directly with the bank, although we've done it both ways (often without actually changing banks). The best way to do it yourself is simply identify comparable home loans and any special rates. While bigger banks will generally match each other, keep in mind you'll likely have more problems using a small lender's rate as your comparison. I personally like the convenience of keeping all my banking together so I steer clear of the small lenders anyway. Another thing to keep in mind with any advertised rate is it's unlikely to be their best offer, with each lender having access to 'under the counter' offers or discount delegations should they need them.

If you are offered a better deal at another bank, make sure you weigh up the financial benefits against the inconvenience of moving all of your banking (direct debits, credit cards etc) which can be extremely time consuming. Also you might not get the same standard of customer service at the new bank. To achieve the best outcome simply negotiate a better rate or mortgage structure with your existing bank. They have teams dedicated to 'saving' mortgages, although this is generally only when you have officially asked to discharge (cancel) your loan. Sometimes you need to take it that far to get the better deal (banks know it's a pain to move so leverage this). However, be prepared for the bank to call your bluff and have a backup plan if they do.

Things to watch out for when switching your mortgage:

- Make sure the interest rate (and discount) being offered isn't a honeymoon rate that reverts to a higher rate after a certain period

- Compare all costs, not just interest rates, because there are also varying upfront, ongoing and exit fees. The comparison rate can be helpful here

- Compare the features too - you don't want to move to a mortgage that doesn't have the features you value in your current one

57% of Aussies don't know their current home loan rate

More than just a better rate

You can also refinance your mortgage for the purpose of accessing additional funds using the equity in your home. This is different to accessing extra repayments you might have made and relates to increasing your total loan limit to access additional funds for a significant life event such as a renovation, a wedding or even a deposit for an investment property. Again, the bank will usually work to a maximum LVR of 80% meaning the new limit will be 80% of the property value.

For example:

> **2012: Property purchased for $500,000 (20% deposit, $400,000 loan)**
>
> **2016: Property valued at $600,000 ($380,000 loan)**

Based on this example the new loan limit will be $480,000 giving you access to an additional $100,000 (subject to being able to afford the new repayments).

Other reasons for refinancing include changing to interest only repayments to lighten the load for a short period or switching mortgage type (from a variable rate to a fixed rate mortgage or vice versa when your fixed rate expires). It's also possible to consolidate your debt (such as credit card or personal loans) into your mortgage. Mortgages have much lower interest rates than credit cards and personal loans so you can save money, although you will pay interest over the life of the loan so you need to make sure you pay the loan back quickly to limit the total interest paid.

CHAPTER SIX
EQUITY

You can use equity
for many things,
but I've only ever
used it to renovate or
purchase investment
property

Equity

Why it's so powerful.

Equity is the difference between the value of an asset and what you owe on it. For example, a property worth $500,000 with a $300,000 mortgage has $200,000 equity. This is the amount of money you would expect to have left over if you sold it (excluding any costs of sale). As you pay a debt down and/or the value of the property increases so too does the equity.

Banks will allow you to access a portion of your equity as property is generally seen as a 'safe' asset. So you can use it for holidays, a car or even another property, assuming you are able to afford the increased loan repayments. Like most things in life though, it's not free and there are restrictions.

You learned about an LVR (Loan to Value Ratio) earlier.

LVR = total borrowings divided by the property value
E.g. $300,000/$500,000 = 60% LVR

Equity is the reverse of an LVR. Where an LVR is the percentage you owe, equity is the percentage you own.

Equity = property value minus total borrowings
E.g. $500,000 - $300,000 = $200,000
(40% expressed as a percentage)

The banks prefer an LVR to be under 80% so they'll only let you access 80% of your equity, and then you need to show you can pay the new mortgage balance back. I've only ever used equity to renovate or purchase investment property, which brings us to our next topic.

Property investing

Risk vs. Reward.

E quity opens up the option to purchase additional property for investment purposes. A lot of people see property investment as risky, especially after periods of high capital growth. They point to 'market corrections' and 'greed', and they're not wrong. There are clear risks, but in my view you can reduce these by taking a measured and patient approach.

Having said that, the purpose of this chapter isn't to convince you to invest in property - there are plenty of books and seminars which aim to do that. I simply want to give you a high level view of the basics so you can form your own view.

Capital growth or cash flow?

There are two key objectives in property investment - capital growth and cash flow. While both are great you generally can't maximise them for the same property.

A focus on capital growth means you are looking to make your money from an increase in the property's value over time. Even if the property is costing you money each year (negative gearing) your aim is to make more back in capital growth. Negative gearing occurs when the cost of owning a property is greater than the income it generates. This creates a taxable loss, which in Australia can be offset against other income including your wage or salary, to provide tax savings.

A focus on cash flow means you aim to make money on the property every year (positive gearing). This occurs when the rent covers all of the property costs (mortgage repayments, maintenance, rates, insurance etc.) and generates an income.

It's possible for a positively geared property to benefit from capital growth, but generally not as much as properties in higher demand areas. Conversely, it's common for higher value properties (often in the larger cities) to be negatively geared. Larger cities are where more of the jobs are, meaning stronger population growth and more pressure on housing. While rents are higher, growth hasn't kept pace with house prices which has pushed the 'yield' down and in many cases resulted in a negative cash flow situation. While both have their risks I have always taken the capital growth approach and done what I can to minimise the gap between incoming rent and the mortgage payments. I believe if you buy in a big city it's more difficult to go wrong over the long term.

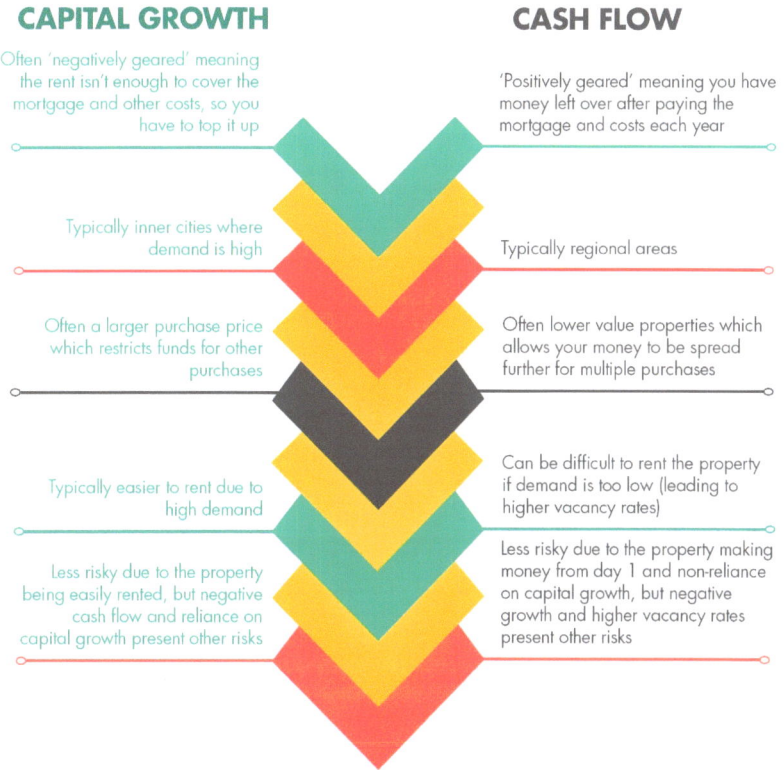

CAPITAL GROWTH

CASH FLOW

Often 'negatively geared' meaning the rent isn't enough to cover the mortgage and other costs, so you have to top it up

'Positively geared' meaning you have money left over after paying the mortgage and costs each year

Typically inner cities where demand is high

Typically regional areas

Often a larger purchase price which restricts funds for other purchases

Often lower value properties which allows your money to be spread further for multiple purchases

Typically easier to rent due to high demand

Can be difficult to rent the property if demand is too low (leading to higher vacancy rates)

Less risky due to the property being easily rented, but negative cash flow and reliance on capital growth present other risks

Less risky due to the property making money from day 1 and non-reliance on capital growth, but negative growth and higher vacancy rates present other risks

Take a ten year view

One of the most common objections to property investment is the potential to buy a property and see either no growth or negative growth in its value. In this case, the investor has 'lost' money. While true on paper, just like shares, you don't realise any physical gains or losses until you sell. There is a saying "It's about time in market, not timing the market". For me, any time you're looking to buy and sell within two or three years, with the hope of capital gain, is speculation. Any market can dip for that period of time, or even longer but history has shown us it is rare for a property in a major city to be worth less today than it was 10 years ago.

Inflation usually does its job as the mortgage doesn't change while everything else becomes more expensive. There are caveats of course. Detroit had a population of 917,000 in 2007 but property values had halved by 2016, along with the population declining to 670,000. But then Detroit was just one of many cities in America heavily dependent on a single industry. Cities like Sydney and Auckland are major markets in their countries, supported by a wide range of industries, whereas Perth, Western Australia saw property value declines due to a slow down in the mining industry it was dependant on.

Detroit Median Sale Price

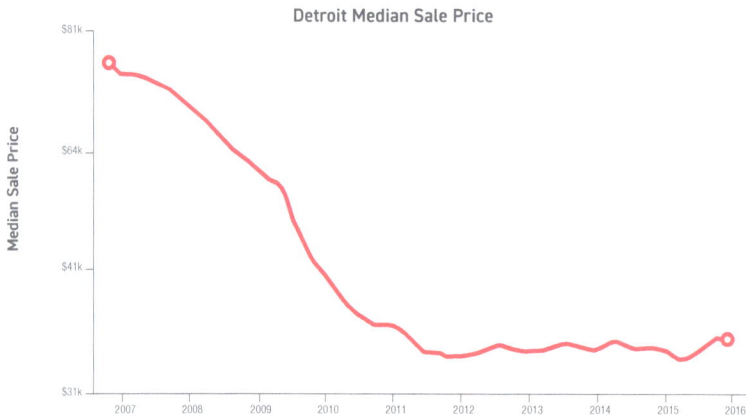

Chart credit: Zillow

But what about all the interest you pay?

It's true that over the lifetime of a loan you end up paying a lot more than the initial loan amount - at interest rates of 6% you pay back more than double! As mentioned earlier, 7% - 8% is about the average rate paid in Australia over the 30 years between 1982 and 2011.

However, you have incoming rental income and negative gearing benefits (as at 2017 in Australia), plus the power of inflation.

Let's work through an example of a property purchased for $500,000 with a $100,000 (20%) deposit and $400,000 loan over 30 years at an interest rate of 7% with repayments paid fortnightly. To be realistic we'll use a yield of 2.9% which would make the property negatively geared (the yield being the return you get from the investment each year, expressed as a percentage). As we're unsure if negative gearing will remain available in the future I have excluded these benefits from the calculations (even though they are very significant).

Over 30 years the total net cost of purchasing the $500,000 property is $333,014 plus the initial $100,000 deposit = $433,000. If the property experiences 0% growth in value there is a $67,000 gain, taxable at 30% (higher depending on your personal situation) leaving $47,000.

Historical Standard Variable Home Loan
Interest Rates Last 30 Years - Australia

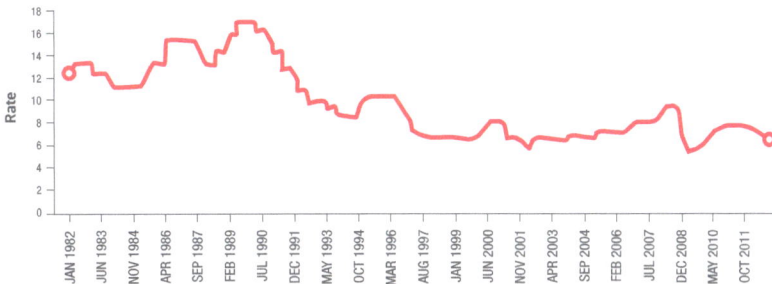

Chart credit: Loansense.com.au

	OUTGOINGS	INCOMINGS
Loan repayments at 7% principal + interest	$820,186 ($420,180 interest)	
Rental income at $300 p/w for 48 weeks of the year (2.9% return) and 3% inflation increase p.a.		$685,056
Ownership costs: Rates, maintenance, insurance etc @ $80 p/w and 3% inflation	$197,914	
TOTAL	**$1,018,100**	**$685,086**

The payments covering the gap between the incoming rent and the outgoing mortgage payments and ownership costs works out to be $11,000 per year ($213 per week). This may be a strain but you can look for a cheaper property or something closer to cash flow neutral or even positively geared.

We are of course not considering the opportunity cost of the initial $100,000 used for the deposit and the extra $11,000 per year. Over 30 years with a healthy 5% p.a. return and 30% tax the initial $100,000 would become $280,679, while $11,000 per year would generate an additional $587,000. So the term deposit option would require $100,000 deposit plus $330,000 ($11,000 per year), totaling $430,000 and deliver $867,000. This would leave a net gain of $437,000, compared to just $47,000 for the property.

So the term deposit wins comfortably when the property grows at 0% but how does it compare when the property increases in value?

Factoring in long term property growth

If the property value simply keeps up with inflation and grows at 3% each year over 30 years it will be worth $1.18 million in that time. As an investment property there would be capital gains tax to pay on the sale of the property of about $200,000 plus the agents fees to sell it so the net figure would be around $800,000 post sale (again we are simplifying the example here by ignoring negative gearing tax benefits). Factoring in the initial $100,000 deposit and $330,000 extra payments leaves a net gain of $370,000 compared to $437,000 for the term deposit.

It's true that past value growth isn't necessarily a reflection of future growth but Australian property grew 7.25% per year between 1985 and 2015[11]. In the above example, if the growth rate averaged 5% p.a. the property value would be $2.1 million with tax to pay of about $500,000 and around $1.5 million in your hand post sale (a net gain of just over $1 million).

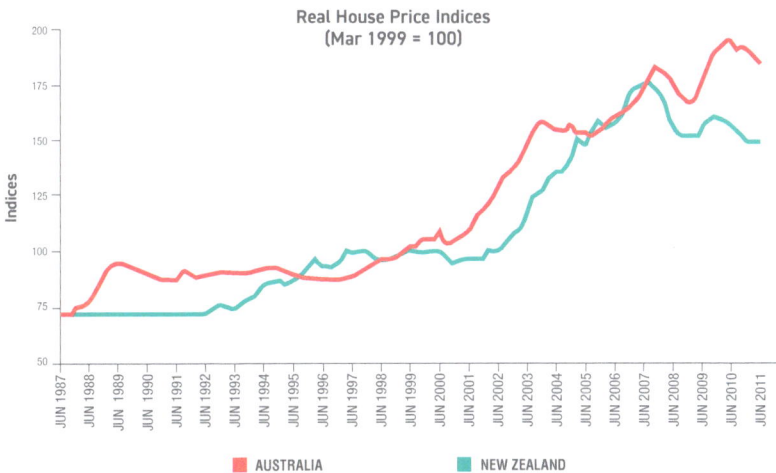

Real House Price Indices
(Mar 1999 = 100)

AUSTRALIA   NEW ZEALAND

Chart credit: ABS, REINZ, RBNZ, macrobusiness.com.au

The point I'm making here is that even if the property gets 0% growth over three decades you will still make a return on the initial $100,000 while anything just over 3% will out perform a healthy term deposit.

11: https://www.rba.gov.au/publications/bulletin/2015/sep/pdf/bu-0915-3.pdf

INVESTMENT OPTION	NET RETURN (AFTER TAX)
Term deposit	$437,000
Property with no growth	$47,000
Property with inflationary growth (3% p.a.)	$370,000
Property with below average growth (5% p.a.)	$1,000,000

But what if the interest rate is higher?

Taking a long term view doesn't mean there aren't risks and by far the worst one is increasing interest rates. In the example we used the long term average of about 7%. Here is how much extra you'd be paying over 30 years if the rates averaged 10%, 12% or 15% over that period (again with fortnightly repayments).

INTEREST RATE	OUTGOINGS	EXTRA INTEREST
7%	$820,186 ($420,180 in interest)	
10%	$956,436 ($556,436 in interest)	$136,000
12%	$1,017,237 ($617,237 in interest)	$200,000
15%	$1,071,091 ($671,091 in interest)	$250,000

At an average 10% interest over 30 years, an additional $136,000 in interest repayments are required (averaging around $4500 per year). This still leaves a healthy overall return but does put large pressure on repayments, especially as we have had periods like the mid to late 1980s where interest rates reached these levels for the better part of a decade. It's a genuine risk and all I can say here is to factor a healthy interest rate buffer into your calculations so you have some room to move should this happen for an extended period of time. Also start small and maybe look to share the first investment with others.

But you're overlooking the risk of tenants.

Tenants do represent a risk. They can miss rent payments, trash your place or worse still, you might not have a tenant at all. One of the reasons we favour investing in major centres is the much lower risk of a vacant property. There is simply more demand for housing. When you combine that with a tidy, warm, safe property with rent set at or slightly below market rate we have (to date) had no problems. We also have landlord insurance covering the building and loss of rent which we see as the cost of our peace of mind. Throughout the years we have installed things like carpet and heat pumps at the request of tenants because we see it as a two way relationship. This helps reduce turnover and also makes the property more attractive should you need to find new tenants.

Sure, you can keep your money in your pocket and maximise returns but we prefer this style of investing and truly believe in karma.

Throughout the years we have installed carpet and heat pumps at the request of the tenants because we see it as a two way relationship

Air BnB

Most of you will have heard of Air BnB but are you using it to generate additional income from your property? It's a great way to make some extra cash to fund your holiday or pay off your mortgage faster.

Friends on the Northern Beaches advertise their home year round and move out to go camping as needed. It might be inconvenient, but when you're getting $500 or more per night in the summer it can be lucrative. Other couples without children offer their spare bedroom throughout the year while we have friends that Air BnB'd their home out while they were on a six month holiday. We do it when we go back to New Zealand to visit family and it covers all our flights.

Our experience with Air BnB'ing our unit lead to Brady creating Key Exchange which provides Air BnB hosts a concierge service for their tenants. This includes meeting them with the keys, checking them in and setting the place up for the next tenants.

CHAPTER SEVEN
ADVICE

Paying for invaluable advice

had a safe but humble upbringing and this meant Mum was always looking to save money buying whatever was cheapest. It certainly made sense as she didn't really have a choice, but one thing I have learned is the value of quality advice. It's one of those things that only becomes obvious with experience as it's difficult to understand why you should pay more for a service which appears largely the same regardless of who you use.

Accountant

Shortly after moving to Sydney we used H&R Block (a chain of tax accountants) to lodge our annual tax returns. They were efficient enough and did make some basic claims for us, but the following year we had an accountant recommended to us.

The additional cost of his service was a few hundred dollars more, but he literally saved us thousands of dollars. We still use him today for more complex issues and he is one of the most important people in our life.

Mortgage Broker

When a broker sells a loan they receive a percentage of the balance up front and then a 'trail' fee for each year the loan stays at the bank. Knowing this, I used to negotiate my mortgage rates directly with the bank thinking that by cutting out the broker I would have more chance of getting a better rate. This all changed when a lender at an Australian bank cost us the chance to purchase a home. A real estate agent had previously recommended a broker so I called him the next day and was blown away by the experience.

Everything was covered via email and phone or he'd come out to us. He didn't just look at rates, but the different lending policies of the banks (for example whether they count a contracting role as a permanent employee in the application) and how it would be best to set the loan up from a tax perspective.

On top of that, he got a better rate than I could. There are two reasons for this experience: 1) He brings a lot of business to the bank so even though he costs them money, he's more valuable to them than a single customer like me; 2) he provides a much higher level of service than a bank employee because he doesn't get paid unless you take out the mortgage.

Property Manager

A lot of investors manage their own properties, and if you have the time it's a sound option. For us though, our Property Manager is invaluable, especially as we live in Australia and the rentals are in New Zealand. She handles everything, including inspections, maintenance, and communications with tenants. She also inspects properties we're looking to purchase and manages any renovations. Things happen quickly because she has established relationships with tradespeople that value her like the banks value our mortgage broker. She charges 7% of our gross rent, which is tax deductible and this means we can spend that time together as a family or identifying additional opportunities.

If a good agent can get you 5% more for your property, it's worth paying them an extra 0.5% commission

Lawyer

We have separate lawyers in Australia and New Zealand and they both provide the same key benefit - peace of mind. For example, our lawyer in Australia managed to identify an important issue in a duplex property we had an offer accepted on. He realised that the 'unit entitlement' (which is like the number of shares you have in the building) worked out to a 49.5% and 50.5% split. It was a legacy thing which had been set up like that for decades but it effectively gave the decision making power to the other owner. Safe to say we walked away as we didn't want to put ourselves in that position (despite the agent's assurances it would be 'ok'). Our New Zealand lawyer has also negotiated smaller deposits or shorter/longer settlements on our behalf.

Real Estate Agent

As covered earlier, when you're selling your property it's tempting to select the agent who charges the lowest commission, or even try to sell the property yourself. On the surface that makes sense, but it also assumes all agents are created equal. Better agents will specialise in one suburb, have experience and importantly a ready made database of buyers from previous open homes they have held. They value their reputation more than a quick sale and rely on referrals from happy customers more than pamphlet drops in your letterbox. When the difference in a commission might be 0.5% of the sale price this is the amount a good agent needs to lift your sale price by to justify their premium. For example selling a house at $700,000 would net you $687,400 after a commission of 1.8% (excluding any other sale costs). If a good agent gets you 5% more ($735,000) and then takes 2.3% you are left with $718,095, which is $30,695 more. With a good prospect list and the right skills a good agent can sell your property for much more than an average agent and they will likely sell it faster for you too.

CHAPTER EIGHT
CONCLUSION

Is property for everyone?

No, I don't think so, but its an option for most of us.

The purpose of this book isn't to convince you to buy property. Its intention is to guide those who would like to buy a home or investment property, and improve their chances of achieving these goals. I also hope I've provided helpful tips to existing home owners looking to pay off their mortgage and/or upgrade to a larger home as their family grows.

There is a lot of expectation in Australia and New Zealand for people to get on the property ladder, with some seeing it as a birth right. I guess it partially comes back to the great 'Aussie/Kiwi dream' and by all accounts this still exists for the vast majority of people. However, property affordability in Australia and New Zealand has never been worse, that's a fact. There has been mountains of commentary on this topic with everyone having an opinion.

To summarise, here is mine:

- Unfortunately, property has never been within reach of everyone. You need a steady income and many people don't have this, whether they are students, unemployed or on very low incomes. Also, some of those with the required income may prioritise travel, renting an inner city location, or a higher lifestyle (going out, buying goods etc.) and that's their choice.

- It is however, still within reach of the vast majority of income earners that want it - but you need to be disciplined and creative. The 'discipline' component is the 'go to' position for many current home owners (often the baby boomers). But as Gen X and Y point out, this alone is not enough which is true. This is where creative thinking is needed, using some of the suggestions I've made in this book.

- So its really up to you. Work out your priorities, and if property is number one then set yourself an achievable goal and go for it. Good luck!

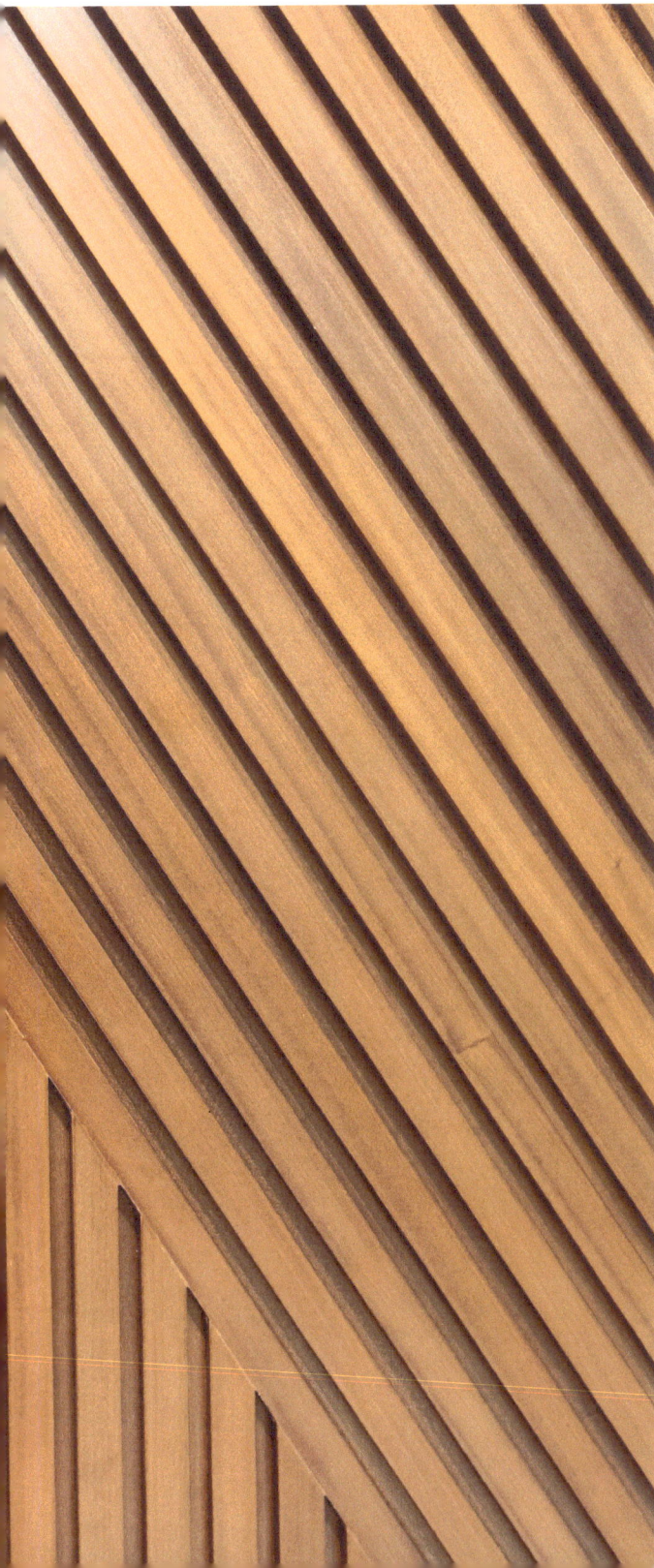

CHAPTER NINE
GLOSSARY

AFFORDABILITY

Calculated by comparing property values to household income presented as a ratio.

AUCTION

A method of sale where all offers occur at the same time at a specific place.

AVERAGE DAYS ON MARKET

The average time it takes to sell property in a particular area.

AVERAGE VENDOR DISCOUNTING

The difference between the original asking price and the actual sale price of a property.

AVM (AUTOMATED VALUATION MODEL)

A computer generated estimate of a property's current value.

BUBBLE

A large increase in property prices fueled by demand and speculation. If demand decreases at the same time supply increases, prices drop sharply and the bubble bursts.

CAPITAL GROWTH

Relates to the increase in value of a property over time. The current value of a property is compared to the amount originally paid for it presented as a percentage or a whole number.

CASH FLOW

Where you aim to make money on the property every year (positive gearing). This occurs when the rent covers all of the property costs (mortgage repayments, maintenance, rates, insurance etc.) and generates an income.

CLEARANCE RATES

The proportion of auctions resulting in a sale.

COMMISSION

A fee charged by the real estate agent to successfully sell the property, usually an agreed percentage of the sale price. Also relates to the fee a broker receives from the bank when they sell a mortgage.

COMPARABLES

Properties of similar size and location as the target property that have either recently sold or are currently for sale.

COMPARISON RATE

Makes different interest rates comparable by factoring in upfront, ongoing and exit fees on mortgages. It also considers what the mortgage reverts to if there is a honeymoon rate.

DEPOSIT

The amount of cash needed to secure a mortgage on a property, usually 20% of the purchase price (leaving 80% financed by the mortgage).

DEVELOPMENT APPROVAL (DA)

Approval needed to undertake development to a property such as a new build, extension or significant renovation. It includes the plans for the location and design of the building to ensure neighbouring properties are consulted and council regulations are followed.

EQUITY

The difference between the value of an asset and what you owe on it. For example, a property worth $500,000 with a $300,000 mortgage has $200,000 equity.

FIXED INTEREST RATE

The interest rate, and therefore the repayments, won't change for a specified period.

GROSS YIELD

The return investors get from a property. It is simply the annual rent divided by the property value.

HONEYMOON RATE

A discounted interest rate that reverts to a higher rate after a certain period.

INFLATION

The rate at which prices for goods and services is rising and, consequently, the purchasing power of currency is falling.

INTEREST ONLY PAYMENTS

Repayments only cover the interest to stop the loan size from increasing. The principal is not repaid.

LENDERS MORTGAGE INSURANCE (LMI)

Insurance premium which enables the buyer to borrow up to 95% of the property value.

LOAN TO VALUE RATIO (LVR)

Total borrowings divided by the property value, expressed as a percentage. For example, borrowings of $300,000 for a property worth $500,000 reflect an LVR of 60%.

MEDIAN

Similar to the average, but simply orders all of the numbers from highest to lowest and takes the middle number.

MEDIAN SALE PRICE

How much you'd expect to pay for a middle of the road property in a particular area. For example, if the median sale price in Sydney is $1 million you would expect half of the properties to be worth less than $1 million and half to be worth more.

MEDIAN PRICE CHANGE

The change in the median sale price over a period of time, expressed as a percentage.

NEGATIVE CAPITAL GROWTH

A reduction in property value over time.

OFFSET ACCOUNT

A transactional account linked to your mortgage. Any money in the transaction account is 'offset' against your mortgage balance, reducing the interest payable.

OVERCAPITALISING

When the cost of a renovation outweighs the value it adds to the property.

PRINCIPAL

The original amount borrowed in a mortgage.

PRINCIPAL AND INTEREST PAYMENTS

Repayments cover both the interest and original principal so that no money is owed at the end of the loan term.

PRIVATE TREATY

A method of sale where the vendor sets an asking price and negotiates with prospective buyers (via the agent).

PROPERTY SHARE

Allows you to share the cost of buying a home with family or friends, while retaining individual control of your finances.

PROPERTY STAGING

Interior designers who put together a presentation plan for your home ready for sale and provide furniture and miscellaneous items.

REFINANCE

Changing the structure of a mortgage or the provider of it in an attempt to access additional funds, reduce interest rates and/or switch loan type.

SETTLEMENT PERIOD
Usually around six weeks but can be as short or as long as you like - although it needs to be agreed with the buyer presale.

SPECULATION
Buying property in the hope of capital gains.

SPLIT RATE MORTGAGE
A mix of both variable and fixed rates mortgages.

STAMP DUTY
A tax due in the transfer of property, payable by the purchaser.

SUPPLY AND DEMAND
The balance between the amount of property available for sale (supply) and the number of buyers (demand).

TAX DEDUCTIBLE
Costs which are able to be deducted from your taxable income, lowering the amount of tax to be paid.

UNIT ENTITLEMENT
The proportion of a unit's share of ownership of the strata scheme. It determines voting rights, share of costs and common property.

VACANCY RATE
The percentage of available rental properties that are vacant at a particular time.

VARIABLE MORTGAGE RATE
The interest rate can change; and if it does, the repayments might too.

YIELD
The return provided by the investment each year, expressed as a percentage.

FOLLOW US

See what others are saying about property in Australia and New Zealand

Join the Property for under 40s Facebook group
https://www.facebook.com/under40sproperty

Follow us on Twitter
https://twitter.com/under40property

Connect with us on LinkedIn
https://au.linkedin.com/in/paulargus